Office for Disarmament Affairs
New York, 2024

The United Nations
DISARMAMENT YEARBOOK 2023

Volume 48

COVER DESIGN: Symbolizing hope and enduring resilience, the ginkgo tree stands as a witness to history—over 150 survived the 1945 atomic bombings in Japan. Its leaves, seen in the background, evoke the steadfast pursuit of a future where legacies of human destruction might give way to growth and lasting peace.

TIMELINE PHOTOS:
The Deputy Minister of Foreign Affairs of Belarus, Yury Ambrazevich (on screen in the photo), addresses the Conference on Disarmament on 28 February, in Geneva. (Credit: UN Photo/Violaine Martin)

Staff members of the United Nations Regional Centre for Peace, Disarmament and Development in Latin America and the Caribbean celebrate the first International Day for Disarmament and Non-Proliferation Awareness, in Lima.

The General Assembly approves the Arms Trade Treaty on 2 April 2013. (Credit: UN Photo/Devra Berkowitz)

The High Representative for Disarmament Affairs, Izumi Nakamitsu (left in the photo), addresses the Disarmament Commission on 3 April. Next to her is Akan Rakhmetullin, Permanent Representative of Kazakhstan to the United Nations. (Credit: UN Photo/Loey Felipe)

Left to right: The Vice-Chair (Maritza Chan (Costa Rica)) and the Chair (Albrecht von Wittke (Germany)) of the Open-ended Working Group to elaborate a set of political commitments as a new global framework that would address existing gaps in through-life ammunition management.

The Secretary-General's Advisory Board on Disarmament Matters at United Nations Headquarters, New York, in June.

On 10 July, Fernando Arias, Director-General of the Organisation for the Prohibition of Chemical Weapons (OPCW), and Bonnie Jenkins, Under Secretary for Arms Control and International Security of the United States, mark the completion of the destruction of the country's declared chemical weapons stockpile. (Credit: OPCW)

The Secretary-General, António Guterres, launches his policy brief, *A New Agenda for Peace*. (Credit: UN Photo/Manuel Elías)

Available in electronic format at
https://yearbook.unoda.org and
https://disarmament.unoda.org.

UNITED NATIONS PUBLICATION
405 East 42nd Street, S-09FW001
New York, NY 10017
United States of America

Email: publications@un.org
Website: shop.un.org

Sales No. E.24.IX.3
Print ISBN: 9789210031608
PDF ISBN: 9789211064841

Copyright © 2024 United Nations
All rights reserved worldwide

Printed in the United States

ACKNOWLEDGEMENTS

Volume 48 of the *United Nations Disarmament Yearbook*, like previous editions, was a collaborative effort to which the staff of the Office for Disarmament Affairs devoted considerable time and effort. It was prepared under the overall direction of the High Representative for Disarmament Affairs, Izumi Nakamitsu, and the Director of the Office, Adedeji Ebo. We sincerely thank all colleagues who contributed to this publication on behalf of other funds, programmes, entities and organizations.

Editor-in-Chief: Diane Barnes

Graphic design and layout: Cecile Salcedo

Writers and contributors:

Kena Alexander
Nora Allgaier
Ismail Balla
Tania Banuelos
Tomisha Bino
Katja Boettcher
Virginia Browning
Tam Chung
Amanda Cowl
Courtney Cresap
Asa Cusack
Radha Day
Razy Aman Eddine
Estela Evangelista
Sylvain Fanielle
Daniel Feakes
Aude Feltz
Julia Freese
Ivor Fung
Claudia Garcia Guiza
Melanie Gerber
Sophie Guillermin-Golet

René Holbach
Jiayi Huang
Shuxin Huang
Rebecca Jovin
Erika Kawahara
Alexandra Kiss
Soo Hyun Kim
Christopher King
Peter Kolarov
Yukimi Kubo
Kathryn Kuchenbrod
Hermann Lampalzer
Alice Marzi
Tak Mashiko
Hideki Matsuno
Silvia Mercogliano
Jiaming Miao
Annelisa Miglietti
Laurie Mincieli
Marykate Monaghan
Ana Moruja Nigro
Suzanne Oosterwijk

Charles Ovink
James Pettit
Katherine Prizeman
Mohamad Reza
Cecile Salcedo
Damon Shavers
Fiona Simpson
Michael Spies
Gizem Sucuoglu
Olga Tegay
Frida Thomassen
Christine Uhlenhaut
Soledad Urruela
Juliana Helou van der Berg
Xiaoyu Wang
Ziwen Xie
Anselme Yabouri
Yue Yao
Melissa Yi
Aaron Junhoung Yoo

GUIDE to the user

The United Nations Office for Disarmament Affairs publishes the *United Nations Disarmament Yearbook* as a **concise reference tool** for diplomats, researchers, students and the general public on disarmament, non-proliferation and arms control issues under consideration by the international community.

The Office is releasing the present **condensed version** of the 2023 *Yearbook*, available in PDF and website formats, to provide an **easy-to-read overview** of the publication earlier in the year. The **full version**, with more comprehensive chapters on the year's activities, will be published on the website **in September 2024**.

The *Yearbook* is **divided into the main multilateral issues** under consideration throughout the year. It includes **developments and trends**, a convenient issue-oriented **timeline** and explanatory **graphics** and charts. The annex on **resolutions, status of treaties and other resources** is a one-stop shop for accessing recommended databases, publications and information materials from the year. The Disarmament Resolutions and Decisions Database contains the resolutions and decisions of the seventy-eighth session of the General Assembly, as well as their sponsors, voting patterns and other related information. The Disarmament Treaties Database provides the status of multilateral regulation and disarmament agreements. The information in those databases was formerly published each year within the *Yearbook*; producing it in database form offers *Yearbook* users a more interactive experience and easier access to data from previous years.

The *Yearbook* website is user-friendly—accessible on **mobile devices** and available in **multiple languages** through third-party machine translation. Official translations in the six official languages of the United Nations will be uploaded as they become available.

Because much of the background information is condensed, consulting **previous editions** for expanded historical knowledge will be helpful.

Websites of United Nations departments and specialized agencies, intergovernmental organizations, research institutes and non-governmental organizations are referenced as **hyperlinks in the online version** of the *Yearbook*.

Symbols of United Nations documents are composed of capital letters combined with figures. Hyperlinks to these documents are included in the online version of the *Yearbook*. Alternatively, they can be accessed, in the official languages of the United Nations, from https://documents.un.org.

Specific disarmament-related documents are also available from the disarmament reference collection at https://library.unoda.org.

CONTENTS

- **1** — Foreword
- **2** — Multilateral disarmament timeline: Highlights, 2023
- **5** — **Developments and trends, 2023**
  1. Nuclear disarmament and non-proliferation — 7
  2. Biological and chemical weapons — 17
  3. Conventional weapons — 25
  4. Regional disarmament — 31
  5. Emerging, cross-cutting and other issues — 37
  6. Gender and disarmament — 43
  7. Disarmament machinery — 51
  8. Information and outreach — 57

- **65** — Annex: **Resolutions, status of treaties and other resources**
  - Disarmament resolutions and decisions of the seventy-eighth session of the United Nations General Assembly — 66
  - Status of multilateral arms regulation and disarmament agreements — 67
  - Publications and other information materials in 2023 — 68
  - Events held on the margins of the 2023 session of the First Committee — 73

Infographics

Figure 1.1	Estimated annual reduction in global nuclear warhead stockpiles	11
Figure 2.2	Secretary-General's Mechanism: nominated qualified experts, expert consultants and analytical laboratories by region (as at December 2023)	21
Figure 2.3	Trends in confidence-building measures: participation of States parties in the Biological Weapons Convention's confidence-building measures, 1987–2023	22
Figure 3.1	World military expenditure by region, 1988–2023	28
Figure 4.2	Timeline of the Conference on the Establishment of a Middle East Zone Free of Nuclear Weapons and Other Weapons of Mass Destruction	34
Figure 5.1	Intergovernmental bodies addressing information and communications technologies security, 2004–present	40
Figure 5.2	A New Agenda for Peace: recommendations for action	41
Figure 6.1	Percentage of women speakers in multilateral disarmament forums, 2021–2023	46
Figure 6.3	Activities of the Office for Disarmament Affairs with a gender perspective	48
Figure 7.1	From consensus to contention: tracking shifts in the General Assembly's disarmament decision-making over the years	53
Figure 7.2	Advisory Board on Disarmament Matters: a diverse body of experts	55
Figure 8.1	Empowering global youth: disarmament outreach by the United Nations in numbers	60
Figure 8.2	Charting progress: the global reach of online disarmament education	61

Maps

Figure 1.2	Worldwide locations of nuclear weapons	13
Figure 2.1	OPCW-designated laboratories (as at November 2023)	20
Figure 4.1	States parties of nuclear-weapon-free zone treaties	33
Figure 6.2	Disarmament in national action plans on women, peace and security	47

"Throughout 2023, disarmament advocates around the world demonstrated **remarkable resilience** in the face of multiplying crises and threats.

Izumi Nakamitsu
High Representative for Disarmament Affairs"

FOREWORD

Welcome to the enhanced preview edition of the 2023 *United Nations Disarmament Yearbook*. The *Yearbook*, now in its forty-eighth volume, provides a comprehensive and authoritative overview of recent developments and trends in the field of disarmament, non-proliferation and arms control, including the relevant activities and achievements of the United Nations and other actors. The aim of this early-release publication is to share key findings from the *Yearbook* at an earlier stage and provide a concise exploration of disarmament-related developments and trends from 2023.

Throughout 2023, disarmament advocates around the world demonstrated remarkable resilience in the face of multiplying crises and threats, from the ongoing conflicts in various regions and the escalation of nuclear tensions, to the proliferation of conventional weapons and the emergence of new technologies with destabilizing potential. Recognizing the interlocking nature of these and other global challenges, the Secretary-General issued his policy brief, *A New Agenda for Peace*, in July. This policy brief offered action-oriented recommendations to help Member States to integrate the tools of multilateral disarmament—including measures to regulate, reduce, or eliminate and destroy weapons—into an anticipated global consensus on tackling current and future problems. The Secretary-General also proposed that those tools, with their proven value in preventing conflict, could and should be used in support of broader efforts to advance our collective peace and security and achieve the 2030 Agenda for Sustainable Development.

Meanwhile, the United Nations Office for Disarmament Affairs undertook new initiatives in pursuit of a more peaceful and secure world. For example, the Office launched the Youth Leader Fund for a World Without Nuclear Weapons, offering 100 scholarships for young people in dozens of countries to develop their skills as change-makers for a nuclear-weapon-free world. My Office also launched its Leaders to the Future workshop series, empowering 55 young advocates to explore how disarmament, non-proliferation and arms control are linked with other matters vital to maintaining international peace and security.

Such efforts, with their aim of nurturing a new generation of disarmament advocates and thinkers, might be likened to the seeds of the *hibakujumoku*—the ginkgo trees renowned for surviving the atomic bombings of Hiroshima and Nagasaki. Thanks to recent efforts, saplings from those trees are now growing all around the world, serving as inspiration for the abolition of nuclear weapons and a future free from the scourge of war. It is my hope that the *United Nations Disarmament Yearbook*, as the definitive guide to developments in our field, will provide similar inspiration and historical perspective to all those committed to the cause of disarmament and the creation of a more peaceful and secure world for all.

Izumi Nakamitsu
Under-Secretary-General
High Representative for Disarmament Affairs
June 2024

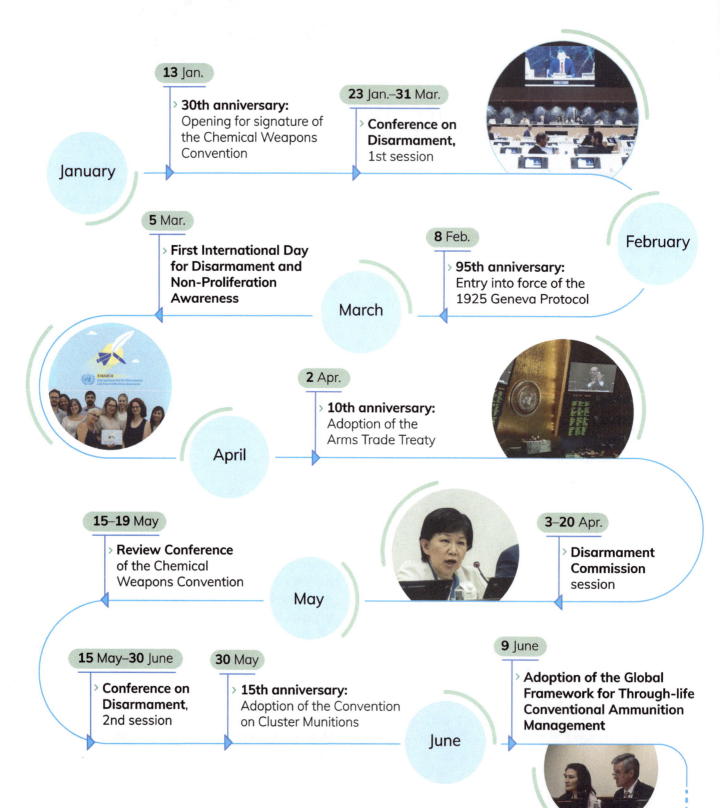

Highlights, 2023
MULTILATERAL disarmament timeline

January

13 Jan. — 30th anniversary: Opening for signature of the Chemical Weapons Convention

23 Jan.–31 Mar. — Conference on Disarmament, 1st session

February

8 Feb. — 95th anniversary: Entry into force of the 1925 Geneva Protocol

March

5 Mar. — First International Day for Disarmament and Non-Proliferation Awareness

April

2 Apr. — 10th anniversary: Adoption of the Arms Trade Treaty

3–20 Apr. — Disarmament Commission session

May

15–19 May — Review Conference of the Chemical Weapons Convention

15 May–30 June — Conference on Disarmament, 2nd session

30 May — 15th anniversary: Adoption of the Convention on Cluster Munitions

June

9 June — Adoption of the Global Framework for Through-life Conventional Ammunition Management

30 June
> **45th anniversary:** Establishment of the Secretary-General's Advisory Board on Disarmament Matters

1 July
> **55th Anniversary:** Adoption of the Nuclear Non-Proliferation Treaty
> **25th anniversary:** Entry into force of the Inter-American Convention against the Illicit Manufacturing of and Trafficking in Firearms, Ammunition, Explosives, and Other Related Materials

July

7 July
> Completion of the **destruction of all declared chemical weapons stockpiles**

20 July
> **Launch** of the Secretary-General's policy brief, *A New Agenda for Peace*

28 Sept.–3 Nov.
> **Seventy-eighth session** of the First Committee of the General Assembly

31 July–15 Sept.
> **Conference on Disarmament**, 3rd session

September

October

5 Oct.
> **45th anniversary:** Entry into force of the Convention on Environmental Modification Techniques

10 Oct.
> **60th anniversary:** Entry into force of the Partial Test Ban Treaty

28 Nov.
> **20th anniversary:** Adoption of the Protocol on Explosive Remnants of War to the Convention on Certain Conventional Weapons (Protocol V)

November

2 Dec.
> **40th anniversary:** Opening for signature of the Convention on Certain Conventional Weapons

December

2023
DEVELOPMENTS
and trends

Eliminating nuclear weapons remains the United Nations' highest disarmament priority. We will not rest until the nuclear shadow has been lifted once and for all.

António Guterres
Secretary-General of the United Nations

1 Nuclear disarmament and non-proliferation

Disarmament Fellows visit a monitoring station of the Preparatory Commission for the Comprehensive Nuclear-Test-Ban Treaty Organization, in September.

NUCLEAR DISARMAMENT and non-proliferation

The year 2023 began with experts moving the hands of the "Doomsday Clock" to 90 seconds to midnight, reflecting their view that human civilization was at its closest to a cataclysmic tipping point in the clock's seven-decade history. That symbolic representation of existential danger stemmed in large part from growing fears about the use of nuclear weapons.

The trend of heightened nuclear risk continued in 2023 owing to six key interlinked trends and occurrences:

> The ongoing war in Ukraine
> The conflict in Gaza
> The increasing tension between nuclear-weapon States, including in the Asia-Pacific, coupled with ongoing qualitative improvements of nuclear arsenals and fears about a return to nuclear arms racing
> The failure to revive the Joint Comprehensive Plan of Action on the

nuclear programme of the Islamic Republic of Iran

> Further progress by the Democratic People's Republic of Korea in improving its nuclear capabilities

> The growing nexus between conventional weapons, new domains and nuclear weapons.

Those trends and occurrences combined not only served to raise nuclear risks—for example, through veiled threats to use nuclear weapons, the possibility of escalation in regional conflicts, and growing opportunity for mistake and miscalculation—but also diminished prospects for strengthening the disarmament and non-proliferation regime. Worse, they contributed to the further erosion of existing instruments and hard-won norms against the use, testing and proliferation of nuclear weapons. In November, the High Representative for Disarmament Affairs reflected on the situation: "We have witnessed nuclear threats in multiple acute crises. The instruments of the cold-war-era arms control regime have either crumbled away or are in acute danger of doing so. We appear to have reached the end of a decades-long trend of declining sizes in nuclear arsenals worldwide. Agreement in disarmament meetings … seems increasingly difficult to find."

The impact of the Russian invasion of Ukraine continued to be reflected both in fears about the use of a nuclear weapon and in strained relations across the nuclear disarmament and non-proliferation regime. Russian officials still issued veiled threats regarding the potential use of nuclear weapons, although less frequently than in 2022. The Russian Federation also "suspended" its participation in the Treaty between the United States of America and the Russian Federation on Measures for the Further Reduction and Limitation of Strategic Offensive Arms (New START Treaty), including that Treaty's verification mechanisms, albeit with a stated intention to strictly comply with the Treaty's quantitative restrictions. The Treaty is the last bilateral arms control agreement on nuclear weapons.

On 25 May, the Russian Federation and Belarus announced that they were formalizing the deployment and storage of Russian non-strategic nuclear weapons in Belarusian territory. In December, Belarus stated that the Russian Federation had completed a shipment of non-strategic nuclear weapons to Belarusian territory. The issue of nuclear sharing and the stationing of nuclear forces outside of national territory continued to be a point of contention in multilateral forums, with critics charging that such arrangements—especially those of the North Atlantic Treaty Organization (NATO)—were inconsistent with the Treaty on the Non-Proliferation of Nuclear Weapons (Nuclear Non-Proliferation Treaty). In August, a non-governmental organization highlighted excerpts of United States budget documents that indicated a possible return of United States nuclear weapons to the United Kingdom. Both the United States and the United Kingdom refused to comment on the matter.

Without directly referencing the conflict in Ukraine, the Russian Federation withdrew its ratification of the Comprehensive Nuclear-Test-Ban Treaty, significantly damaging prospects for the Treaty's entry into force and undermining the norm against nuclear testing. The withdrawal further exacerbated concerns raised by civil society about a potential return to nuclear explosive testing in the light of increased activity at test sites in China, the Russian Federation and the United States. Nevertheless, membership numbers of the Treaty continued to rise among non-nuclear-weapon States, with Solomon Islands and Sri Lanka ratifying the agreement and Somalia signing it in 2023.

In her statement to the Conference on Facilitating the Entry into Force of the Comprehensive Nuclear-Test-Ban Treaty (Article XIV Conference), the High

Representative for Disarmament Affairs stated: "It is deeply concerning to hear ... about potential backtracking on non-testing pledges. A return to nuclear testing would lead us to another age of instability, taking us closer to the edge of catastrophe, damaging human health and our environment in the process ... In today's climate of growing nuclear danger, I call on all States that have previously declared moratoriums on nuclear testing to reaffirm these moratoriums and to take immediate steps to sign and/or ratify the [Comprehensive Nuclear-Test-Ban Treaty]."

The conflict in Ukraine remained a significant point of contention in the review process of the Nuclear Non-Proliferation Treaty, especially in relation to the protection of the Zaporizhzhia Nuclear Power Plant and threats to use nuclear weapons. Throughout the year, the International Atomic Energy Agency (IAEA) expressed concern regarding the situation at the Zaporizhzhia facility and called for the observance of the Agency's Seven Pillars for ensuring nuclear safety and security in an armed conflict. In November, the Director General of IAEA advised that six of the Pillars were compromised at the facility either fully or partially, especially those related to staffing at the site, the conduct of regular maintenance activities and special measures taken for securing a stable cooling water supply. More broadly, the conflict continued to exacerbate tensions between States within the disarmament and non-proliferation regime, leading to acrimonious disputes over procedure and affecting efforts to implement relevant treaties and other instruments.

As noted, decreasing trust and resurgent competition between nuclear-weapon States also contributed to the rise in nuclear risk and diminished efforts to pursue nuclear disarmament. The United States and its allies pressed their allegations regarding the rapid expansion by China of its nuclear arsenal and fissile material production capability. In one report, the United States Department of Defense alleged that China possessed 500 operational nuclear warheads. China continued to refute the allegation, asserting that the onus was on both the United States and the Russian Federation to lead in the process of nuclear arms reduction. China also pushed back strongly against calls for it to announce a moratorium on the production of fissile material for nuclear weapons purposes, stating that such moratoriums were unverifiable and unfairly biased towards larger nuclear-weapon States.

As calls for enhanced transparency by China mounted in various multilateral forums, so too did calls within the United States to expand its nuclear stockpile to meet its challenge of two near-peer nuclear-weapon States. The Congressional Commission on the Strategic Posture of the United States, a group of bipartisan experts, stated in a report that the United States needed a nuclear posture capable of simultaneously deterring both China and the Russian Federation. It also called for, inter alia, an increase in the number of available platforms for delivering nuclear weapons. With the ongoing development by the Russian Federation of novel nuclear delivery systems not constrained by any agreement, experts expressed concern that the post-cold-war trend of declining global nuclear weapons numbers was ending, after more than three decades.

Adding further to nuclear risk in the Asia-Pacific region, in 2023 the Democratic People's Republic of Korea continued its nuclear and ballistic missile programmes by conducting 31 test launches using ballistic missile technology—fewer than in 2022, but with five trials of intercontinental ballistic missiles. The country also successfully put its first military satellite into orbit in November, after two failed attempts, in May and August. In addition, the Democratic People's Republic of Korea amended its Constitution in September to enshrine its nuclear policy, which significantly lowered its threshold for the potential use of nuclear weapons. Leaders from the country also

Nuclear disarmament and non-proliferation

Figure 1.1
Estimated annual reduction in global nuclear warhead stockpiles

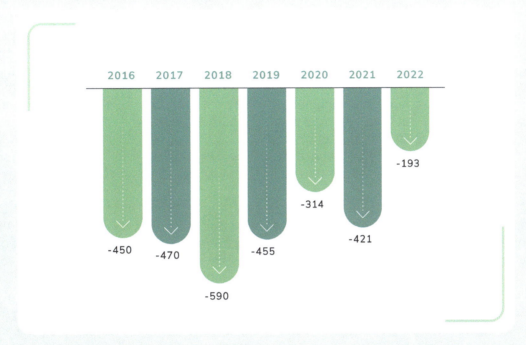

Although thousands of nuclear warheads have been destroyed since the 1980s, the annual reduction in global stockpiles has decreased significantly.

NOTE: The numbers shown are of total stockpiles, not of active military stockpiles.
DATA SOURCE: SIPRI yearbooks from 2017 to 2023; and Federation of American Scientists, Nuclear Information Project.

held a summit with Russian counterparts, where they agreed to strengthen their collaboration in military matters. The Security Council convened nine times in response to the repeated violations of its relevant resolutions, but the body remained divided over taking further punitive action.

Anxiety about nuclear weapons was once again prevalent in the Middle East in 2023, with the war in Gaza serving to raise the spectre of their use and dampen prospects for either a resolution to the issue of the Iranian nuclear programme or the achievement of a zone free of nuclear weapons and all other weapons of mass destruction in the region. An unofficial comment in which an Israeli cabinet minister suggested Israel could use nuclear weapons in the conflict drew condemnation from States across the region and beyond.

Efforts to revive the Joint Comprehensive Plan of Action on the Iranian nuclear programme fell short once again. The remaining parties to the Plan and the United States achieved no gains in a new round of the Vienna Talks, while the Islamic Republic of Iran expanded its nuclear programme in both size and expertise. In June, the media reported on indirect talks between the United States and the Iranian Government aimed at reaching an informal deal that allegedly would have included, inter alia, a commitment from the latter to cease enrichment of uranium to or beyond 60 per cent, in exchange for the release of frozen Iranian assets and an exchange of prisoners. Despite a temporary drop in the country's enrichment of uranium to 60 per cent, it had reverted to the higher rate of production by the end of December. Throughout 2023, IAEA reported that the Islamic Republic of Iran had continued to engage in several activities inconsistent with the Plan of Action, including enrichment of uranium to 60 per cent, 20 per cent and 5 per cent, and creating a stockpile well above the Plan's limits (GOV/2023/57).[1] IAEA also detected highly enriched uranium particles containing up to 83.7 per cent U-235. However, following several meetings, it stated that it "had no further questions on the matter at that stage".

The year saw several attempts to increase monitoring and verification of the Iranian nuclear programme, as reflected in a joint statement issued in March by IAEA and the Atomic Energy Organization of Iran. Nevertheless, IAEA reiterated its position that its verification and monitoring had been seriously affected by the cessation of Iranian nuclear-related commitments under the Plan. Furthermore, IAEA said that the situation had worsened because of a subsequent Iranian decision to remove all of the Agency's Plan-related surveillance and monitoring equipment.

For its part, the Islamic Republic of Iran continued to refute allegations that it was pursuing a nuclear weapons programme, contending that its activities were consistent with its commitments under the Nuclear Non-Proliferation Treaty. Meanwhile, several non-governmental organizations calculated that the State had acquired enough fissile material for multiple nuclear weapons. Adding to regional proliferation concerns, in September, Saudi Arabia reaffirmed that should the Islamic Republic of Iran acquire nuclear weapons, it would do so as well.

In 2023, the nuclear-weapon States maintained their rhetorical commitment to a world free of nuclear weapons, including at the first meeting of the Preparatory Committee for the 2026 Review Conference of the Parties to the Nuclear Non-Proliferation Treaty. However, those States continued programmes to qualitatively improve their nuclear arsenals, including through the development of new delivery systems. China, the Russian Federation and the United States progressed in the modernization of all three legs of their nuclear triads.

Meanwhile, the United States announced plans to deploy its B61-12 nuclear gravity bomb to European allies in 2024. The variant is considered an upgrade, as its new tail fin allows for greater accuracy. The United States also announced the development of the B61-13 gravity bomb—intended to be used against "harder and large-area military targets" and to allay concerns about the retirement of the B83-1 and the W87-1—which would be the first completely new nuclear warhead manufactured by the United States in over three decades. Although the President of the United States did not request any funding for a nuclear-armed, submarine-launched cruise missile in 2024, the United States Congress allocated funding for the proposed weapon in the 2024 National Defense Authorization Act.

---

[1] Owing to the Islamic Republic of Iran ceasing its implementation of the additional protocol to its comprehensive safeguards agreement and other voluntary transparency measures under the Joint Comprehensive Plan of Action since February 2021, IAEA could only estimate the size of the Iranian enriched uranium stockpile based on information provided by the country.

Nuclear disarmament and non-proliferation

Figure 1.2
Worldwide locations of nuclear weapons

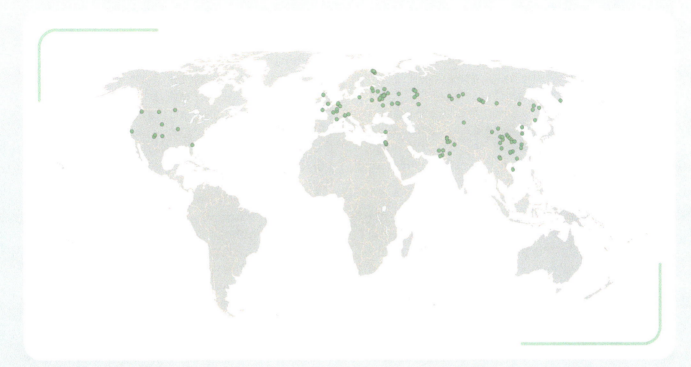

This map of nuclear weapons locations includes sites where there is reason to believe that nuclear weapons probably are deployed or stored, and those where nuclear weapons and their components are designed, fabricated and assembled or dismantled. The list of locations is incomplete; locations for the Democratic People's Republic of Korea are unknown from open sources. Most States that possess nuclear weapons do not release information about locations of nuclear weapons and nuclear components.

The boundaries and names shown and the designations used on this map do not imply official endorsement or acceptance by the United Nations. A dotted line represents approximately the line of control in Jammu and Kashmir agreed upon by India and Pakistan. The final status of Jammu and Kashmir has not yet been agreed upon by the Parties. Final boundary between the Sudan and South Sudan has not yet been determined.

BASE MAP SOURCE: United Nations Geospatial

DATA SOURCE: Federation of American Scientists, Nuclear Information Project

Non-governmental sources assessed that China continued to develop three new missile silo fields for intercontinental ballistic missiles and was developing new variants and other advanced strategic delivery systems. China reportedly further expanded its dual-capable intermediate-range ballistic missile force, refitting its Type 094 ballistic missile submarines with the longer-range JL3 submarine-launched ballistic missile, while also reassigning an operational nuclear mission to its bombers and developing an air-launched ballistic missile that might have nuclear capability.

The Russian Federation progressed with the replacement of legacy nuclear and dual-capable missile systems with newer variants and reportedly deployed a new Yars intercontinental ballistic missile at the Kozelsk base in the Kaluga region, south-west of Moscow, capable of carrying multiple thermonuclear warheads.

The Russian Federation also conducted further deployments, production and testing of novel delivery vehicles, including the Avangard hypersonic weapon and the Poseidon autonomous underwater vehicle. According to non-governmental sources, the country also engaged in the upgrading and replacement of non-strategic nuclear weapons systems.

In addition, the first session of the Preparatory Committee for the 2026 Review Conference of the Parties to the Nuclear Non-Proliferation Treaty took place from 31 July to 11 August. Having skipped the one-year break that traditionally separates review cycles of the Treaty, the States parties revived contentious debates from the 2022 Review Conference on matters that included nuclear propulsion, nuclear sharing, the Joint Comprehensive Plan of Action, transparency around fissile material production and other activities, the protection of nuclear power plants in zones of armed conflict and the fulfilment of article VI of the Nuclear Non-Proliferation Treaty. Divisions over those issues were exacerbated by parallel geostrategic developments, such as the war in Ukraine and tensions in the Middle East and the Asia-Pacific regions.

Despite an enduring articulated commitment by almost all the States parties to the Nuclear Non-Proliferation Treaty and to keeping it fit for purpose, the session was marked by procedural disputes, rancorous debate and frequent uses of the right of reply. As had become customary, the Preparatory Committee could not reach a consensus agreement on a summary of proceedings. The process reached a new low point when one State party refused to support the consensus adoption of a procedural report if the Committee Chair even submitted a draft summary of the proceedings as a working paper, something seen as pro forma in the past.

Despite the divisions affecting the Preparatory Committee, a working group established to discuss and make recommendations to the Preparatory Committee on measures that would improve the effectiveness, efficiency, transparency, accountability, coordination and continuity of the review process of the Treaty had met the week prior (24–28 July), and engaged in positive and constructive dialogue. In particular, the working group productively considered measures to strengthen accountability for the implementation of existing commitments through enhanced and interactive reporting, including in-person, during the review cycle. Although States parties could not agree on consensus recommendations or next steps, there was general agreement that they had made good progress that should be built upon.

The second Meeting of States Parties to the Treaty on the Prohibition of Nuclear Weapons was another bright spot in 2023. Although the Treaty remained in its nascency with a relatively small membership, the meeting highlighted work by States parties to find practical, ethical and scientific approaches to achieving a world free of nuclear weapons. The participants made progress in efforts to assist victims of nuclear weapons use and testing, to lay the groundwork for a competent international authority that could verify nuclear disarmament, and to ensure the inclusion of diverse stakeholders in the Treaty's implementation. States parties adopted a declaration that unequivocally rejected the logic of nuclear deterrence and decried any and all threats to use nuclear weapons (TPNW/MSP/2023/14, annex I). In her remarks during the meeting, the High Representative for Disarmament Affairs reflected, "Important work has been done to implement the Treaty on the Prohibition of Nuclear Weapons. This is especially welcome considering the stagnant progress or backsliding that we are currently witnessing in other parts of the disarmament and non-proliferation architecture."

Although entrenched divisions around nuclear weapons featured prominently in the deliberations of the First Committee of the General Assembly, the body's session in 2023 included two notable highlights. The first was the adoption by a large majority of General Assembly resolution 78/240, entitled "Addressing the legacy of nuclear weapons: providing victim assistance and environmental remediation to Member States affected by the use or testing of nuclear weapons. By that resolution, the General Assembly recognized the responsibility of Member States that had used or tested nuclear weapons to address the harm caused to victims. States also encouraged further international cooperation and discussions to assist victims and to assess and remediate environments contaminated by the use and testing of nuclear weapons and other nuclear explosive devices.

Regarding the second highlight, as part of efforts to revive prospects for a treaty banning the production of fissile material for nuclear weapons and other explosive devices, the General Assembly included in its annual resolution on the matter, resolution 78/28, a call for the Secretary-General and the High Representative for Disarmament Affairs to facilitate engagement between States that possess or produce fissile material for nuclear weapons or other nuclear explosive devices on transparency and confidence-building measures with a view to launching negotiations.

"

Chemical weapons are an abomination. They have no place in our world. ... We must make every effort to eliminate these senseless weapons of terror. In the name of the victims of these attacks—and as a deterrent to future chemical warfare—those responsible for any use must be identified and held accountable for their crimes.

António Guterres
Secretary-General of the United Nations

"

2 Biological and chemical weapons

The Youth for Biosecurity fellows learned about the laboratories with biosafety levels 3 and 4 (BSL-3 and BSL-4) designations, at the Spiez Laboratory on 9 August.

BIOLOGICAL AND CHEMICAL
weapons

In 2023, the Organisation for the Prohibition of Chemical Weapons (OPCW) continued to deliver on its mandate and commitment to ensuring the full and effective implementation of the Convention on the Prohibition of the Development, Production, Stockpiling and Use of Chemical Weapons and on Their Destruction (Chemical Weapons Convention). OPCW marked several milestones during the year, including the inauguration and immediate start of operations of its Centre for Chemistry and Technology (ChemTech Centre), the convening of the fifth special session of the Conference of the States Parties to review the operation of the Chemical Weapons Convention (fifth Review Conference), and the end of the destruction of all declared chemical weapons stockpiles.

The year also marked one decade since OPCW began addressing the chemical weapons dossier in the Syrian Arab Republic. The organization's Technical Secretariat continued to make efforts to ensure that the Syrian Government resolved all gaps, inconsistencies and discrepancies that had arisen from the initial declaration of its chemical weapons programme. Since April 2021, the Technical Secretariat has attempted, without success, to organize the twenty-fifth round of consultations between the OPCW Declaration Assessment Team and the Syrian National Authority. That was owing to, inter alia, the Syrian Arab Republic's refusal to issue a visa to the lead technical expert of the Declaration Assessment Team. In October, however, after two and a half years of delays, the Syrian Arab Republic finally issued visas to all members of the Declaration Assessment Team, and the twenty-fifth round of consultations was held in Damascus in November. The OPCW Fact-Finding Mission maintained its work to establish the facts surrounding allegations of chemical weapons use in the Syrian Arab Republic. The OPCW Technical Secretariat issued a report of the Mission on 28 June regarding incidents of alleged use of toxic chemicals in Kharbit Massasneh, Syrian Arab Republic, on 7 July and 4 August 2017 (S/2186/2023). Likewise, the OPCW Investigation and Identification Team kept up its activities to identify the perpetrators of chemical weapons use in the country, pursuant to the decision of the Conference of the States Parties adopted on 27 June 2018 (decision C-SS-4/DEC.3). The OPCW Technical Secretariat issued a report of the Investigation and Identification Team on 27 January 2023 focusing on an incident in Douma, Syrian Arab Republic, on 7 April 2018 (S/2125/2023).

While OPCW completed its critical work of verifying the destruction of the remaining declared chemical weapons stockpiles in July, it ramped up its article VI chemical industry inspections despite the remaining impact of the coronavirus disease (COVID-19) pandemic.

In its efforts to build capacities among States parties to prevent the re-emergence of chemical weapons, the OPCW Technical Secretariat delivered, through strong engagement with States parties, international cooperation programmes via hybrid, virtual or in-person events, some of them conducted at the OPCW ChemTech Centre. That allowed the Technical Secretariat to assist in promoting the peaceful uses of chemistry; advancing scientific and technological cooperation; countering the threats posed by non-State actors; and expanding partnerships with international organizations, non-governmental organizations, the chemical industry and other entities. The OPCW Technical Secretariat also continued to deliver support to Ukraine, upon its request, under article X of the Convention (assistance and protection against chemical weapons).

Additionally, OPCW continued its work to achieve the universality of the Chemical Weapons Convention, urging the remaining States not parties to the Convention to join without delay or preconditions. In October, at a major OPCW capacity-building exercise "CHEMEX Africa", which was jointly organized in Algiers with Algeria, the Director-General of OPCW met with the Foreign Minister of South Sudan. During the meeting, both sides signed a joint communiqué and agreed to cooperate to complete South Sudan's accession process as soon as possible.

The year 2023 was also important for the Convention on the Prohibition of the Development, Production and Stockpiling of Bacteriological (Biological) and Toxin Weapons and on Their Destruction (Biological Weapons Convention), as it marked the start of the 2023–2026 intersessional programme adopted by the ninth Review Conference of the Biological Weapons Convention, in late 2022.

The centrepiece of the new intersessional programme, the Working Group on the strengthening of the Convention, held three sessions in Geneva in 2023. After considering organizational issues at its first meeting, held on 15 and 16 March, the body addressed substantive topics when it subsequently convened from 7 to 18 August and from 4 to

Figure 2.1
OPCW-designated laboratories (as at November 2023)

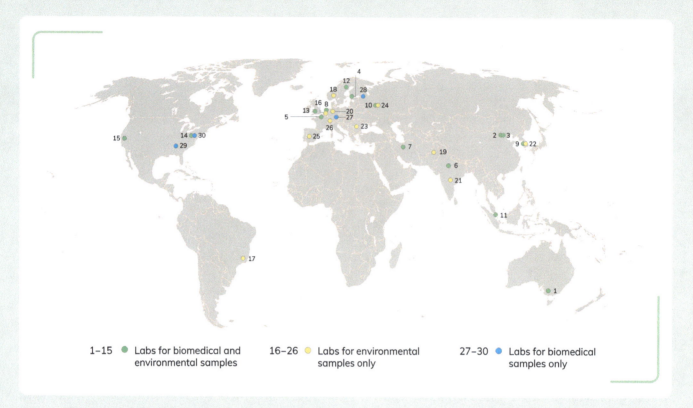

1–15 ● Labs for biomedical and environmental samples
16–26 ○ Labs for environmental samples only
27–30 ● Labs for biomedical samples only

The OPCW network of designated laboratories is a linchpin of the organization's verification regime and its capacity to investigate allegations of the use of chemical weapons. Across the globe, there are currently 30 laboratories designated by the OPCW for the analysis of authentic biomedical and/or environmental samples.

1. Defence Science and Technology Group (Australia)
2. Laboratory of Analytical Chemistry, Research Institute of Chemical Defence (China)
3. Laboratory of Toxicant Analysis, Academy of Military Medical Sciences (China)
4. Finnish Institute for Verification of the Chemical Weapons Convention (Finland)
5. DGA Maîtrise NRBC, Département Analyse Chimique (France)
6. VERTOX Laboratory, Defence Research and Development Establishment (India)
7. Defense Chemical Research Laboratory (Islamic Republic of Iran)
8. TNO Defence, Safety and Security (Netherlands)
9. Chemical Analysis Laboratory, CBR Directorate, Agency for Defense Development (Republic of Korea)
10. Laboratory for the Chemical and Analytical Control of the Military Research Centre (Russian Federation)
11. Verification Laboratory, Defence Medical and Environmental Research Institute, DSO National Laboratories (Singapore)
12. Swedish Defence Research Agency, FOI (Sweden)
13. Defence Science and Technology Laboratory, Porton Down (United Kingdom)
14. DEVCOM Chemical Biological Center, Forensic Analytical Laboratory (United States)
15. Lawrence Livermore National Laboratory (United States)
16. Defensielaboratoria – Laboratoires de la Défense (Belgium)
17. Laboratório de Análises Químicas, Centro Tecnológico do Exército (Brazil)
18. Laboratory for Analysis of Chemical Threat Agents, Norwegian Defence Research Establishment (Norway)
19. Analytical Laboratory, Defense Science and Technology Organization (Pakistan)
20. Bundeswehr Research Institute for Protective Technologies and CBRN Protection (Germany)
21. Centre for Analysis of Chemical Toxins, Indian Institute of Chemical Technology (India)
22. CBRN Defense Research Institute, Republic of Korea Defense Command (Republic of Korea)
23. Research and Innovation Center for CBRN Defense and Ecology, Chemical Analysis Laboratory (Romania)
24. Central Chemical Weapons Destruction Analytical Laboratory of the Federal State Unitary Enterprise, "State Scientific Research Institute of Organic Chemistry and Technology" (Russian Federation)
25. Laboratorio de Verificación de Armas Químicas, INTA Campus La Marañosa (Spain)
26. Spiez Laboratory, Swiss NBC Defence Establishment (Switzerland)
27. Bundeswehr Institute of Pharmacology and Toxicology (Germany)
28. Laboratory of Chemical Analytical Control and Biotesting, Research Institute of Hygiene, Occupational Pathology and Human Ecology (Russian Federation)
29. Centers for Disease Control and Prevention (United States)
30. U.S. Army Medical Research Institute of Chemical Defense (United States)

The boundaries and names shown and the designations used on this map do not imply official endorsement or acceptance by the United Nations. A dotted line represents approximately the line of control in Jammu and Kashmir agreed upon by India and Pakistan. The final status of Jammu and Kashmir has not yet been agreed upon by the Parties. Final boundary between the Sudan and South Sudan has not yet been determined.

BASE MAP SOURCE: United Nations Geospatial
DATA SOURCE: OPCW

Figure 2.2

Secretary-General's Mechanism: nominated qualified experts, expert consultants and analytical laboratories by region (as at December 2023)

The Secretary-General has a mandate to carry out investigations when Member States bring to his attention the alleged use of chemical or biological weapons. To fulfil this mandate, the Secretary-General's Mechanism for Investigation of Alleged Use of Chemical and Biological Weapons was established. Under the Mechanism, a roster of experts and laboratories is maintained. The United Nations relies on countries to fill the roster by designating technical experts to deploy to the field on short notice, as well as analytical laboratories to support such investigations. Member States facilitate further the training of experts and laboratory exercises in close cooperation with the Office for Disarmament Affairs.

Figure 2.3

Trends in confidence-building measures: participation of States parties in the Biological Weapons Convention's confidence-building measures, 1987–2023

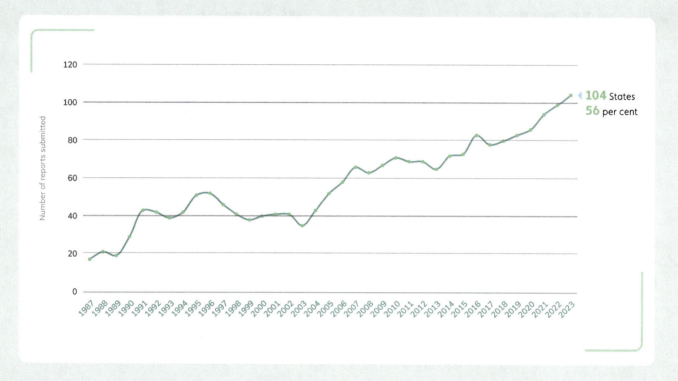

This graph shows the history of submission rates for reports of States parties under the Convention's confidence-building measures system introduced in 1987. While the overall level of participation in the measures has remained low over the years, a positive trend can be seen in recent years. In 2023, a record number of States parties (104) submitted confidence-building measure reports, resulting in a participation rate of 56 per cent.

8 December. Additionally, delegations met from 11 to 13 December for the annual meeting of the States parties.

Despite continued challenging geopolitical circumstances, the Working Group was able to conduct substantive deliberations concerning the strengthening of the Convention and addressed the topics allocated to its 2023 meetings (BWC/CONF.IX/9, chap. II, para. 8). Furthermore, delegates discussed proposals regarding the mechanisms to be established on international cooperation and assistance under article X and on the review of scientific and technological developments. While discussions on the topics allocated to the Working Group remained at an early and conceptual stage, States parties shared a willingness and constructive spirit to make tangible progress by developing concrete recommendations and a road map for the way ahead.

On 15 February, South Sudan acceded to the Biological Weapons Convention, becoming the 185th State party. As at 31 December, four signatory States had not yet ratified the Convention, and eight States had neither signed nor ratified it.[1]

---

[1] Lists of States parties, signatory States and non-signatory States are available at www.un.org/disarmament/biological-weapons/about/membership-and-regional-groups.

Participants of the Biological Weapons Convention Implementation Support Unit's regional workshop on promoting confidence-building measures in South-East Asia gather in Bangkok in October. The workshop was convened in partnership with the United Nations Interregional Crime and Justice Research Institute and the European Union, under its Chemical, Biological, Radiological and Nuclear Risk Mitigation Centres of Excellence initiative.

> We all need to keep pulling together in the same direction: the direction of **saving lives**, as many as we can, and as speedily as we can.
>
> **Izumi Nakamitsu**
> High Representative for Disarmament Affairs

3 Conventional weapons

From 20 to 24 March, the United Nations Regional Centre for Peace and Disarmament in Africa conducted a training workshop for national commissions on combating the proliferation of small arms and light weapons. The workshop, held in Abidjan, Côte d'Ivoire, was organized by the Peace and Security department of the West African Economic and Monetary Union.

CONVENTIONAL weapons 3

The year 2023 saw both positive developments and new challenges in the context of conventional arms. In much of the world, international peace and security continued to suffer from the illicit transfer, diversion, destabilizing accumulation and misuse of small arms and light weapons, as well as their ammunition. In a variety of settings, armed violence and conflict continued to be driven and sustained by the ongoing movement of weapons and ammunition to and between non-State actors, including in the context of organized crime and terrorism.

According to the Stockholm International Peace Research Institute (SIPRI), world military expenditure rose by 6.8 per cent in real terms in 2023, to a total of $2.4 trillion, which amounts to 2.3 per cent of the global gross domestic product and around $306 per capita. Factoring in plans announced by some Member States to boost military budgets in response to the current security landscape, global military spending is estimated to continue to rise sharply in the coming years.

Following the Russian invasion of Ukraine, many States continued to provide military assistance to the Ukrainian armed forces, including transfers of arms and ammunition. Conventional arms transfers included heavy weapons and military equipment, such as armoured combat vehicles, anti-aircraft systems, artillery, helicopters, missile systems and uncrewed combat aerial vehicles, as well as small arms and light weapons and their ammunition. In addition, there were reports of States transferring or planning to transfer weapons to the Russian armed forces. Those weapons were reportedly used in Ukraine and said to include uncrewed aerial vehicles, ballistic missiles and ammunition. On eight occasions in 2023, the Security Council considered the issue of arms transfers, including the risks stemming from violations of the agreements regulating the export of weapons and military equipment.

Harm to civilians and civilian infrastructure also remained a significant concern, with most of the civilian casualties recorded in Ukraine continuing to be caused by explosive weapons with wide-area effects. The attacks included shelling from artillery, tanks, multiple-launch rocket systems, and cruise and ballistic missiles, as well as airstrikes.

Furthermore, the Security Council remained actively seized of threats posed by the misuse, illicit transfer and destabilizing accumulation of small arms and light weapons and their ammunition, particularly in situations of armed conflict and in relation to their potential diversion.

Efforts to implement the 2001 Programme of Action to Prevent, Combat and Eradicate the Illicit Trade in Small Arms and Light Weapons in All Its Aspects, along with its 2005 International Tracing Instrument, continued apace in 2023. Preparations for the fourth Review Conference on the Programme of Action also accelerated.

States achieved a major milestone in comprehensively addressing the threats posed by illicit trafficking, diversion and unplanned explosions of conventional ammunition. The Open-ended Working Group on Conventional Ammunition successfully concluded its work in June, leading to the adoption by the General Assembly of the Global Framework for Through-life Conventional Ammunition Management (A/78/111). That new instrument filled the gap in dedicated regulatory instruments for conventional ammunition at the international level. The SaferGuard programme, managed by the Office for Disarmament Affairs, also continued its efforts to promote the application of the International Ammunition Technical Guidelines to assist States in advancing safe and secure ammunition management.

Meanwhile, the Security Council continued to devote attention to the issue of improvised explosive devices in its thematic discussions and decisions. The Council addressed the matter in relation to various country-specific situations, including in the context of arms embargoes and peace operations.

Additionally, a growing number of Governments participated in two multilateral transparency instruments on conventional weapons. A total of 63 Member States submitted annual reports to the United Nations Report on Military Expenditures during its 2023 reporting cycle, an increase of 50 per cent from 2022. Likewise,

Figure 3.1

World military expenditure by region, 1988–2023

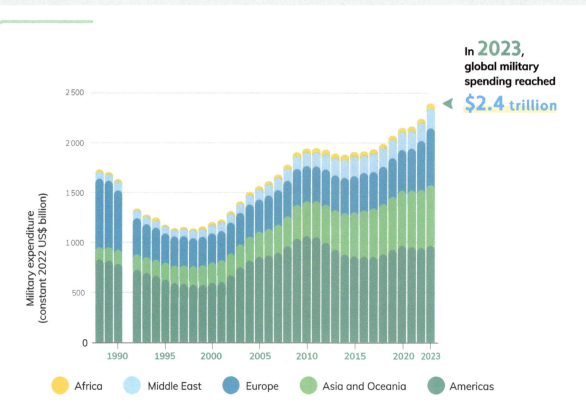

Note: The absence of data for the Soviet Union in 1991 means that no total can be calculated for that year.
Source: SIPRI Military Expenditure Database, April 2023

26,000 people can be treated for malaria for the price of **1 battle tank**.

Source: International Peace Bureau

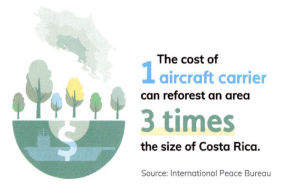

The cost of **1 aircraft carrier** can reforest an area **3 times** the size of Costa Rica.

Source: International Peace Bureau

200,000 children can attend a year of school for the price of **1 stealth fighter**.

Source: Office for Disarmament Affairs, Intro2Disarmament

Conventional weapons

72 States submitted reports to the United Nations Register of Conventional Arms, up from 62 reports in 2022.

The United Nations Trust Facility Supporting Cooperation on Arms Regulation (UNSCAR) funded eight projects aimed at promoting and supporting the implementation of multilateral conventional arms and transparency instruments. As the administrator of the Trust Facility, the Office for Disarmament Affairs provided substantive input for those projects, ensuring their alignment with strategic thematic priorities established by the programme's strategic planning group. In 2023, the Office selected and launched 10 projects from the 50 responses it received to the 2022 annual call for proposals.

OPPOSITE PAGE: Global military expenditure increased to a record $2.4 trillion in 2023. The facts and figures above demonstrate how resources could be invested instead in priority areas such as conflict prevention, health, education and environmental protection.

BELOW: Izumi Nakamitsu, High Representative for Disarmament Affairs, delivers opening remarks in the ministerial-level meeting on the Caribbean Firearms Roadmap in Saint Lucia on 15 November.

Regional frameworks and organizations are **critical building blocks for the networked multilateralism** that is at the heart of the Secretary-General's vision. Successful implementation of these regional approaches requires robust and sustainable partnerships between the United Nations and regional organizations, donors and, of course, civil society.

Izumi Nakamitsu
High Representative for Disarmament Affairs

4 Regional disarmament

Police officers participate in the course on interdicting small arms, ammunition, parts and components, held in Saint Vincent and the Grenadines from 21 to 23 March.

REGIONAL
disarmament

4

In 2023, despite the wars in Ukraine and Gaza exacerbating tensions, regional activities in support of disarmament, non-proliferation and arms control continued to endure. The goals of the year's regional disarmament efforts ranged from preventing the proliferation of weapons of mass destruction to countering the illicit manufacturing of and trade in conventional arms, particularly small arms, light weapons and their ammunition. The United Nations engaged, coordinated and facilitated cooperation with States, regional and subregional organizations, relevant international organizations and civil society, including through exchanges and dialogues, capacity-building projects and information campaigns.

In the field of weapons of mass destruction, three States ratified or signed the Treaty on the Prohibition of Nuclear Weapons. In Latin America and the Caribbean, the Bahamas signed the Treaty. In Africa, Djibouti signed the agreement. In Asia and the Pacific, Sri Lanka acceded to the Treaty. Separately,

Figure 4.1
States parties of nuclear-weapon-free zone treaties

African Nuclear-Weapon-Free Zone Treaty ● State party ● Signatory
Treaty for the Prohibition of Nuclear Weapons in Latin America and the Caribbean ● State party
South Pacific Nuclear Free Zone Treaty ● State party
Treaty on the Southeast Asia Nuclear Weapon-Free Zone ● State party
Treaty on a Nuclear-Weapon-Free Zone in Central Asia ● State party

Nuclear-weapon-free zones strengthen the global nuclear non-proliferation regime, advance the case for global nuclear disarmament, and strengthen both regional and international peace and security. In parallel, nuclear-weapon-free zones are "landmark instruments" that cover roughly half the world's land mass (86 million square kilometres).

The boundaries and names shown and the designations used on this map do not imply official endorsement or acceptance by the United Nations. A dotted line represents approximately the line of control in Jammu and Kashmir agreed upon by India and Pakistan. The final status of Jammu and Kashmir has not yet been agreed upon by the Parties. Final boundary between the Sudan and South Sudan has not yet been determined. A dispute exists between the Governments of Argentina and the United Kingdom of Great Britain and Northern Ireland concerning sovereignty over the Falkland Islands (Malvinas).

BASE MAP SOURCE: United Nations Geospatial
DATA SOURCE: Office for Disarmament Affairs Treaties Database

the Comprehensive Nuclear-Test-Ban Treaty gained two new States parties via ratification by Solomon Islands and Sri Lanka, while Somalia signed the Treaty and the Russian Federation withdrew from it. Albania, the Congo and Zimbabwe ratified or acceded to the International Convention for the Suppression of Acts of Nuclear Terrorism, in August, September and November, respectively. In February, South Sudan acceded to the Biological Weapons Convention.

In the area of conventional weapons, a degree of progress was made in adherence by States to relevant global and subregional treaties. Singapore acceded to the Convention on Certain Conventional Weapons, in September. Nigeria ratified the Convention on Cluster Munitions, in February.

Figure 4.2

Timeline of the Conference on the Establishment of a Middle East Zone Free of Nuclear Weapons and Other Weapons of Mass Destruction

22 Dec. (2018) — The General Assembly **adopts decision 73/546**, requesting the Secretary-General to convene a conference to elaborate a treaty establishing a Middle East zone free of nuclear weapons and other weapons of mass destruction.

18–22 Nov. (2019) — The **first session of the Conference** is held under the presidency of Jordan. Participating States adopt a Political Declaration to demonstrate their firm commitment to establishing a Middle East zone free of nuclear weapons and other weapons of mass destruction.

29 Nov.–3 Dec. — The **second session of the Conference** takes place under the presidency of Kuwait. States decide to establish an informal working committee to take forward their deliberations during the intersessional period.
(UN Photo/Eskinder Debebe)

28 Aug. (2020) — The Conference **postpones its second session** until 2021 owing to the COVID-19 pandemic.

7–9 Jun. (2022) — The **working committee** agrees to invite experts to contribute to discussions.

6–8 Sept. — The **working committee** hears presentations from invited experts on two key topics: legal aspects of a future Middle East zone treaty and verification in relation to nuclear weapons.

15–17 Mar. — The **working committee** hears presentations and discusses both a glossary of terms for the future treaty, as well as its general principles and obligations.

14–18 Nov. — The **third session of the Conference** is held under the presidency of Lebanon. The Conference report included a substantive summary of the deliberations of the Conference.
(UN Photo/Manuel Elías)

14–16 June — The **working committee** continues discussion on both topics from the previous meeting and agrees on a summary of its work.

13–17 Nov. — The **Conference convenes its fourth session** under the presidency of Libya. States adopt new measures to enhance the effectiveness of the working committee.
(UN Photo/Loey Felipe)

ABOUT THE CONFERENCE

- **WHEN?** Annually on the third week of November
- **WHERE?** United Nations Headquarters, New York
- **WHO?**
  - **24 Members to the Conference:** Algeria, Bahrain, Comoros, Djibouti, Egypt, Iran (Islamic Republic of), Iraq, Israel, Jordan, Kuwait, Lebanon, Libya, Mauritania, Morocco, Oman, Qatar, Saudi Arabia, Somalia, State of Palestine, Sudan, Syrian Arab Republic, Tunisia, United Arab Emirates and Yemen
  - **5 Observer States:** China, France, Russian Federation, United Kingdom and United States
  - **3 international organization observers:** International Atomic Energy Agency, Organisation for the Prohibition of Chemical Weapons and Biological Weapons Convention Implementation Support Unit
- **WHAT/WHY?** To elaborate a treaty establishing a Middle East zone free of nuclear weapons and other weapons of mass destruction

Regional disarmament

The fourth session of the Conference on the Establishment of a Middle East Zone Free of Nuclear Weapons and Other Weapons of Mass Destruction was convened at United Nations Headquarters from 13 to 17 November. That meeting represented the commitment of the participating countries to multilateralism and dialogue for improving the current security environment and strengthening regional and international peace and security amid the war in Gaza and its effects on the wider region.

In the meantime, States within existing nuclear-weapon-free zones continued efforts to strengthen those zones in 2023 by enhancing cooperation within and between them, thus contributing to the global nuclear disarmament and non-proliferation regime at the regional level. In particular, States in nuclear-weapon-free zones worked together to ensure full implementation of their respective treaties by building the capacities of their implementation agencies and fully utilizing their consultation mechanisms. Furthermore, those States continued engaging with nuclear-weapon States to resolve outstanding issues regarding assurances against the use or the threat of use of nuclear weapons. In the case of the Treaty on the Southeast Asia Nuclear-Weapon-Free Zone, States parties continued dialogues and discussions with nuclear-weapon States to obtain their signatures or ratifications of the relevant Protocol to the Treaty. In addition, the President of Kazakhstan discussed the importance of the potential ratification by the United States of the Protocol (on negative assurances) to the Treaty on a Nuclear-Weapon-Free Zone in Central Asia.

Meanwhile, the Office for Disarmament Affairs and its three regional centres expanded their engagement with regional and subregional organizations to explore new opportunities and strengthen existing platforms for regional dialogue on security and arms control. As part of that effort, the centres assisted States and regional organizations in acceding to and implementing multilateral and regional treaties and conventions, as well as in further developing capacities to manage conventional weapons and ammunition and combat their illicit manufacturing and trade. For instance, the United Nations Regional Centre for Peace, Disarmament and Development in Latin America and the Caribbean, in partnership with the Caribbean Community's Implementation Agency for Crime and Security, continued implementing the Caribbean Firearms Roadmap, which is aimed at accelerating efforts to prevent and combat the illicit proliferation of firearms and ammunition in the region by 2030. The Regional Centre for Peace and Disarmament in Asia and the Pacific, based in Kathmandu, supported the organization of a regional workshop and seminar on confidence-building measures and the Programme of Action on Small Arms and Light Weapons, and its International Tracing Instrument, while also conducting scoping missions for the Saving Lives Entity (SALIENT), a United Nations funding facility. In Lomé, the Regional Centre for Peace and Disarmament in Africa organized regional seminars on preventing violent extremism, managing conventional weapons and integrating gender-responsive action into small-arms-control measures.

Furthermore, regional and subregional organizations increased their activities to advance a range of disarmament goals. The United Nations supported those organizations by, for example, bolstering its support to the African Union's flagship initiative, "Africa Amnesty Month", as well as a new effort by the Organization of American States to develop a road map for preventing and combating the illicit trafficking of firearms and ammunition.

Let us not only think about where we wish to be in the next twenty-five years, but also the **many steps we must take** along the way to get there. Information and communications technologies will not lie dormant, so neither should our **collective efforts to address associated risks**.

Izumi Nakamitsu
High Representative for Disarmament Affairs

5 Emerging, cross-cutting and other issues

Next-generation artificial intelligence practitioners and students attend a two-day capacity-building workshop on responsible artificial intelligence for peace and security. The training, held in Malmö, Sweden, in November, was organized by the Office for Disarmament Affairs and SIPRI.

EMERGING, CROSS-CUTTING and other issues

In the 2023 sessions of various United Nations bodies, the international community continued to make progress in addressing several emerging challenges related to developments in science and technology and their implications for international peace and security.

On outer space, the Open-ended Working Group on Reducing Space Threats through Norms, Rules and Principles of Responsible Behaviours, established pursuant to General Assembly resolution 76/231, held its final two substantive sessions. Nevertheless, despite holding a wide-ranging discussion,[1] the Working Group was ultimately unable to adopt a final report. The year also included the first substantive session of the Group of Governmental Experts on Further Practical Measures for the Prevention of an Arms Race in Outer Space. Established pursuant to General Assembly resolution 77/250, the Group is mandated to consider and make recommendations on the substantial elements

---

[1] The discussions are reflected in the Chairperson's summary (A/AC.294/2023/WP.22).

of an international legally binding instrument related to the prevention of an arms race in outer space. It is scheduled to hold an additional session in 2024.

In addition, the Disarmament Commission successfully concluded its discussions and adopted recommendations on the practical implementation of transparency and confidence-building measures in outer space activities (for more information, see chap. 7). Reflecting different views on the approach to prevent an arms race in outer space, the General Assembly approved two new open-ended working groups, one mandated to meet from 2024 to 2025 and the other from 2024 to 2028.

Meanwhile, the Open-ended Working Group on Security of and in the Use of Information and Communications Technologies 2021–2025 held its fourth, fifth and sixth substantive sessions and adopted its second annual progress report by consensus (A/78/265). The Working Group agreed, inter alia, to establish a global, intergovernmental directory of points of contact to facilitate State information-sharing and interaction in the event of an information and communications technologies incident, on a voluntary basis.

Member States also continued preparations to negotiate a global digital compact in support of the 2024 Summit of the Future. As the co-facilitators of the relevant intergovernmental process, Sweden and Zambia convened a series of informal consultations and thematic "deep dives" aimed at informing the discussions.

On autonomous weapons systems, the Group of Governmental Experts related to emerging technologies in the area of lethal autonomous weapons systems convened in accordance with a decision of the 2022 Meeting of the High Contracting Parties to the Convention on Certain Conventional Weapons. It adopted a report concluding, among other things, that States must ensure compliance with international law, in particular with international humanitarian law, throughout the life cycle of weapons systems in the area of lethal autonomous weapons systems. In the report, the Group also concluded that States should, when necessary, (a) limit the types of targets that those systems could engage; (b) limit the duration, geographical scope and scale of the operation of the weapon system; and (c) provide appropriate training and instructions for human operators (CCW/GGE.1/2023/2).

On 20 July, the Secretary-General, António Guterres, presented to Member States his policy brief, *A New Agenda for Peace*, outlining his vision for multilateral efforts for peace and security, based on international law, for a world in transition. Framed around the core principles of trust, solidarity and

 Responsible AI for Peace Podcast

> **Episode 1**: "Not so peaceful technology? What risks may civilian AI pose to peace and security?"
> Project leads **Charles Ovink** (Office for Disarmament Affairs) and **Vincent Boulanin** (Stockholm International Peace Research Institute) explore the ways misuse of civilian AI can present risks to international peace and security.

> **Episode 2**: "With Emily Bender, on the risks of large language models and generative AI"
> **Emily Bender**, an American linguist who co-authored one of the most cited articles on the risks posed by large language models, unpacks the relationship between Large Language Models (LLM) and the current hype around Generative AI and discusses the risks of increasing reliance on LLM-based AI tools.

Figure 5.1
Intergovernmental bodies addressing information and communications technologies security, 2004–present

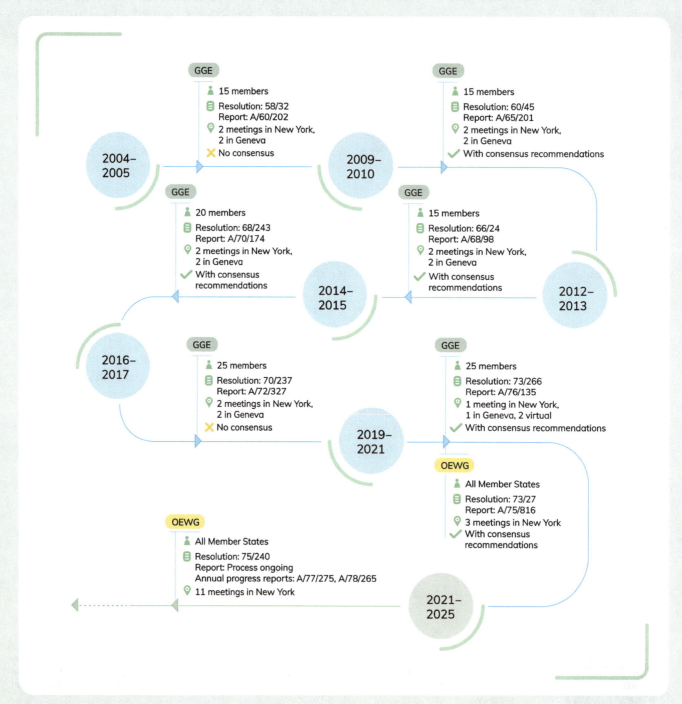

ABBREVIATIONS: GGE, Group of Governmental Experts; OEWG, Open-ended Working Group.

Emerging, cross-cutting and other issues

Figure 5.2

A New Agenda for Peace: recommendations for action

Prevention at the global level: addressing strategic risks and geopolitical divisions

- Action 1: Eliminate nuclear weapons
- Action 2: Boost preventive diplomacy in an era of divisions

Preventing conflict and violence and sustaining peace

- Action 3: Shift the prevention and sustaining peace paradigm within countries
- Action 4: Accelerate implementation of the 2030 Agenda for Sustainable Development to address the underlying drivers of violence and insecurity
- Action 5: Transform gendered power dynamics in peace and security
- Action 6: Address the interlinkages between climate, peace and security
- Action 7: Reduce the human cost of weapons

Strengthening peace operations and addressing peace enforcement

- Action 8: Strengthen peace operations and partnerships
- Action 9: Address peace enforcement
- Action 10: Support to African Union and subregional peace support operations

Novel approaches to peace and potential domains of conflict

- Action 11: Prevent the weaponization of emerging domains and promote responsible innovation

Strengthening international governance

- Action 12: Build a stronger collective security machinery

universality, the document contains 12 recommendations for action across five priority areas. The *New Agenda* characterizes disarmament as a powerful prevention tool that is connected to the attainment of the Sustainable Development Goals. It offers forward-leaning recommendations to a world at crossroads, including for preventing the use and proliferation of nuclear weapons and accelerating their elimination; reducing the human cost of weapons and centring collective efforts on the imperative to save human lives; preventing weaponization of new technologies, including in cyber and outer space, as well as evolving risks linked to advances in biology; stepping up space diplomacy; and seeking ways to address the deadlock in some disarmament institutions. The Summit of the Future, to be held in September 2024, will deliberate "A Pact for the Future", which will elaborate, among other issues, matters relevant to disarmament informed by *A New Agenda for Peace.*

"
One in three women experiences physical and sexual violence in their lifetime. This is more than a social concern; it is an **international security crisis**. The illicit proliferation and misuse of arms **exacerbate this violence**.

Izumi Nakamitsu
High Representative for Disarmament Affairs

"

6 Gender and disarmament

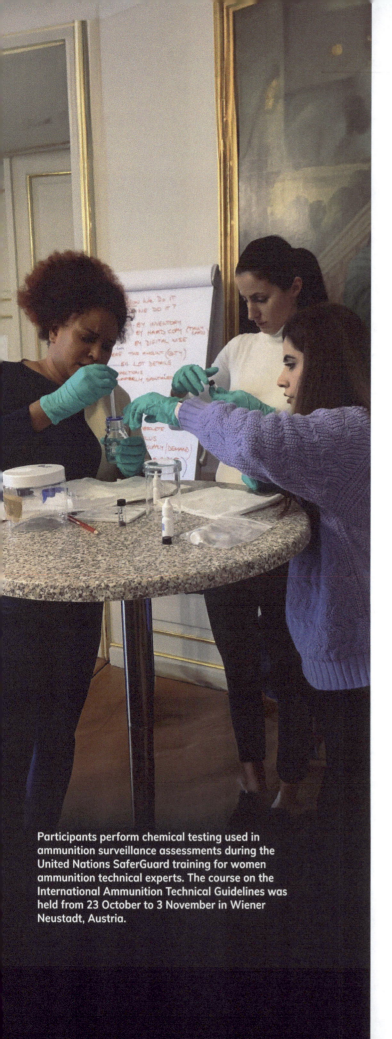

Participants perform chemical testing used in ammunition surveillance assessments during the United Nations SaferGuard training for women ammunition technical experts. The course on the International Ammunition Technical Guidelines was held from 23 October to 3 November in Wiener Neustadt, Austria.

GENDER and disarmament 6

In his policy brief *A New Agenda for Peace*, launched in 2023, the Secretary-General recognized inequalities and patriarchy as root causes of conflict and highlighted how transforming gendered power dynamics sustained peace and prevented violence (action 5). Noting a rising backlash against women's rights, the Secretary-General recommended that States commit to eradicating all forms of gender-based violence through robust and comprehensive legislation, as well as introducing concrete measures to secure women's meaningful participation in peace and security at all levels of decision-making.

In the policy brief, the Secretary-General also recognized the need to foster human-centred disarmament by reducing military expenditures and increasing investments in prevention and social infrastructure, with a strong focus on redressing gender inequalities. In that connection, he asked States to consider allocating 15 per cent of their official development assistance specifically for gender equality, emphasizing the need for sustained, predictable and flexible financing. The Secretary-General also encouraged Governments to devote a minimum of 1 per cent of assistance directly to women's organizations, especially grass-roots groups mobilizing for peace.

In 2023, global military expenditure continued to increase. According to estimates by the United Nations Entity for Gender Equality and the Empowerment of Women (UN-Women), the total amount spent in 2022 was already enough to fund the global implementation of all the gender-related Sustainable Development Goals and targets nearly three times over. Meanwhile, the Secretary-General's Advisory Board on Disarmament Matters called for a more holistic appreciation of security, with more resources spent on gender equality and other global priorities and less spending on weapons (A/78/287).

In 2023, Chile and Colombia declared "feminist foreign policies". During the General Assembly's seventy-eighth session, the 18 States of the Feminist Foreign Policy Plus group[1] reaffirmed their commitment to taking "feminist, intersectional and gender-transformative approaches to ... foreign policies" in the Political Declaration on Feminist Approaches to Foreign Policy.

In some intergovernmental disarmament processes, including for the Treaty on the Prohibition of Nuclear Weapons, the Anti-Personnel Mine Ban Convention and the Convention on Cluster Munitions, dedicated focal points continued to coordinate the integration of a gender perspective and related matters into relevant political processes. Meanwhile, in the seventy-eighth session of the General Assembly, First Committee, 78 States signed a joint statement on gender. Of the 61 disarmament resolutions adopted by the General Assembly in 2023, 38 per cent included language on gender dimensions or women's participation—an increase of 8 per cent from the previous session.

During the Security Council's open debate on small arms and light weapons, held in December under Ecuador's presidency, the Council focused particularly on the linkages between the women, peace and security agenda and the control of small arms and light weapons (S/PV.9509). In briefing the Council, the High Representative for Disarmament Affairs and the Deputy Director of the United Nations Institute for Disarmament Research (UNIDIR) both urged States to support the systematic collection of sex- and age-disaggregated data on the impacts of weapons, among other recommendations. On the margins of the debate, the Council members that were signatories[2] of the Shared Commitments on Women, Peace and Security delivered a joint statement in which they emphasized the impact of small arms and light weapons on women and girls.

Gender-responsive disarmament and arms control also featured as a central topic in the Secretary-General's annual report to the Security Council on women, peace and security (S/2023/725). The Council touched on related concerns during debates on women, peace and security, which it held in March (S/PV.9276 and S/PV.9276 (Resumption 1)) and October (S/PV.9452, S/PV.9452 (Resumption 1) and S/PV.9452 (Resumption 2)).

The Women and Peace and Security Focal Points Network—chaired by Romania and the United States in 2023—recommended increased investment in arms control, non-proliferation and disarmament, among other

---

[1] Albania, Argentina, Belgium, Canada, Chile, Colombia, Costa Rica, France, Germany, Israel, the Kingdom of the Netherlands, Liberia, Luxembourg, Mexico, Mongolia, Rwanda, Spain and Tunisia.

[2] Albania, Brazil, Ecuador, France, Gabon, Japan, Malta, Switzerland, United Arab Emirates, United Kingdom, United States and the incoming members of the Security Council, Guyana, Republic of Korea, Sierra Leone and Slovenia.

Developments and trends, 2023

human security interventions aimed at "creating economic opportunities for women and championing gender equality and women's leadership in all sectors of society, fostering social inclusion, preventing and responding to gender-based violence, and protecting and promoting women's and girls' human rights".

A number of actors further explored the role of arms control in preventing sexual and gender-based violence. In the annual report to the Security Council on conflict-related sexual violence (S/2023/413), the Secretary-General outlined military spending and arms proliferation as key aspects in the prevention of sexual violence in conflict. In the annual Security Council debate on sexual violence in conflict, in July, several States underscored the need to curb the illicit flow of weapons (S/PV.9378 and S/PV.9378 (Resumption 1)). Furthermore, in the biennial report to the Security Council on small arms and light weapons (S/2023/823), the Secretary-General encouraged the Council to mandate United Nations entities to systematically collect gender- and age-disaggregated data on the impact of weapons

Figure 6.1

Percentage of women speakers in multilateral disarmament forums, 2021–2023

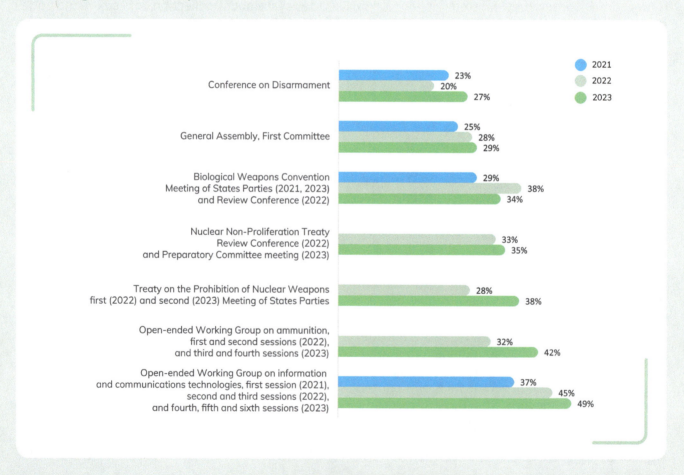

Member States have agreed, through the General Assembly's biennial resolution on women, disarmament, non-proliferation and arms control (77/55), as well as other commitments, to achieve women's equal, full and effective participation in disarmament decision-making. The Office for Disarmament Affairs collects data on speakers in most forums, usually through daily summaries, as a way to measure effective participation. In 2023, the proportion of women representing States providing statements on disarmament increased in some forums.

Figure 6.2

Disarmament in national action plans on women, peace and security

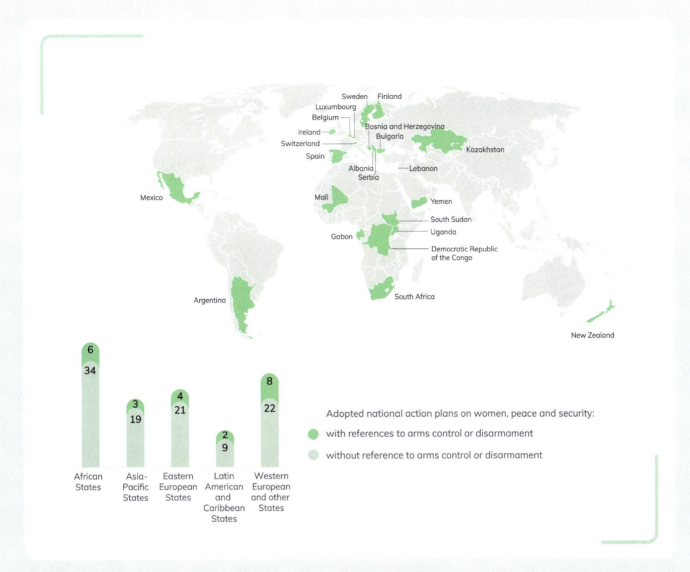

The 23 countries indicated in the map above have adopted national action plans on women, peace and security with references to arms control or disarmament in the monitoring framework. The bar chart shows the number of countries by region.

The boundaries and names shown and the designations used on this map do not imply official endorsement or acceptance by the United Nations. A dotted line represents approximately the line of control in Jammu and Kashmir agreed upon by India and Pakistan. The final status of Jammu and Kashmir has not yet been agreed upon by the Parties. Final boundary between the Sudan and South Sudan has not yet been determined. A dispute exists between the Governments of Argentina and the United Kingdom of Great Britain and Northern Ireland concerning sovereignty over the Falkland Islands (Malvinas).

BASE MAP SOURCE: United Nations Geospatial

and ammunition, both in recording casualties and when monitoring incidents of conflict-related sexual violence.

In 2023, new research by UNIDIR on the role of weapons in conflict-related sexual violence provided options to leverage arms control and disarmament measures in efforts to prevent such violence. The possible measures could include integrating arms-related risks into relevant early-warning mechanisms; collecting and sharing data on conflict-related sexual violence disaggregated by presence of weapons; and considering the risk of such violence when making decisions about arms transfers. The research showed that, in countries

Figure 6.3
Activities of the Office for Disarmament Affairs with a gender perspective

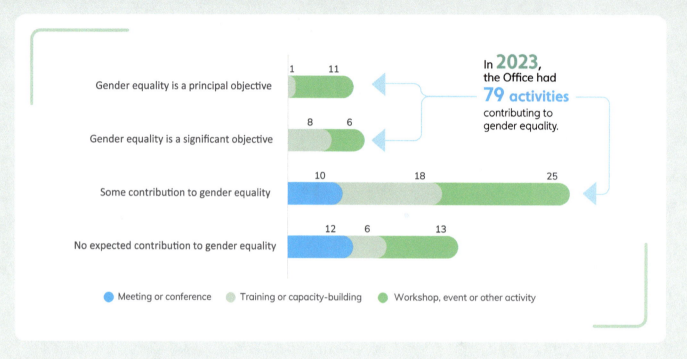

where disaggregated data on weapons were available, between 70 and 90 per cent of incidents of sexual violence in conflict involved weapons, particularly firearms. In December, UNIDIR and the United Nations Action Network against Sexual Violence in Conflict hosted an online event on the role of arms control in preventing sexual violence. Focused on the situation in the Sudan, the event took place during the "16 Days of Activism against Gender-Based Violence" annual global campaign, held under the theme "Invest to prevent violence against women and girls". In addition to the High Representative for Disarmament Affairs delivering a video message, the Office for Disarmament Affairs joined its regional centres and partners, including the International Action Network on Small Arms (IANSA), to publicly highlight the role of arms control in preventing gender-based violence. For example, the United Nations Regional Centre for Peace, Disarmament and Development in Latin America and the Caribbean participated in the Gun Free Valentine campaign organized by IANSA. While the Regional Centre issued Spanish- and English-language social media posts in support of the campaign, IANSA showcased three legal studies in which the Centre cross-referenced firearms legislation and norms on preventing violence against women in States within the Caribbean Community, in or around Central America and in South America.

Another central theme in 2023 was the online dimension of gender-based violence and the use of new technologies. The impact of innovation and technologies on gender equality in the digital age was in focus during International Women's Day, on 8 March, and throughout the sixty-seventh session of the Commission on the Status of Women, from 6 to 17 March. Through the Commission's agreed conclusions (E/2023/27), States recognized that violence, including sexual and gender-based violence and abuse, could occur in digital and online spaces; that the use of artificial intelligence (AI) could have negative impacts on women and girls; and that "targeted measures" should be used to counteract all forms of discrimination against women and girls, including those exacerbated by the use of new and emerging technologies. The Commission brought together more than 7,000 participants in New York, with more than 900 events held on the margins of the session. The High Representative for Disarmament Affairs participated in several related panel discussions, including an event on "Increasing Women's Representation in Cyber and Tech". In 2023, the High Representative also engaged with States at a plenary meeting on "Women in Cyber" during the Singapore International Cyber Week and at the annual Breaking Barriers event on women in science and security, hosted by the Civilian Research and Development Foundation (CRDF Global).

Meanwhile, in the Secretary-General's report on current developments in science and technology and their potential impact on international security and disarmament efforts (A/78/268), particular focus was placed on gender considerations in relation to various types of weapons systems, as well as the equal participation of women and men in related intergovernmental discussions. The report reflected a recognition that the integration of increasingly advanced technologies into the military domain could be used to reinforce, intentionally or not, gender and other social inequalities. The Secretary-General also outlined opportunities and risks in the development of several types of technologies, including AI, which could exacerbate gender bias and discrimination in outcomes based on imbalanced or non-representative data.

Gender-mainstreaming Small Arms Control Training Course

- Self-paced
- Available in **English**, **French**, **Spanish** and **Portuguese** (Arabic to be added)
- Presents the **linkages** between gender and small arms and light weapons
- Raises awareness of **gender issues** among small arms and light weapons practitioners at every level
- Builds **buy-in** regarding how gender awareness makes their work more effective
- Demonstrates why and how to **prevent** armed gender-based violence through gender-responsive small arms control measures

 Learn more and watch the explainer video.

Lamenting the persistent deadlock in parts of the disarmament machinery has become a common refrain ... but the time for lamentation must end. Instead, we must turn our attention to **concrete, sensible solutions**. We must ensure that the machinery is **fit for purpose** so that it can facilitate the management of threats in traditional and new domains and identify solutions.

Izumi Nakamitsu
High Representative for Disarmament Affairs

7 Disarmament machinery

The Conference on Disarmament meets in Geneva, on 28 February. (Credit: UN Photo/ Violaine Martin)

DISARMAMENT
machinery

7

While components of the disarmament machinery remained stagnant in 2023, the year saw some positive developments, particularly around the Disarmament Commission's achievement of consensus recommendations for the first time since 2017. Those recommendations, concerning the practical implementation of transparency and confidence-building measures in outer space activities, came six years after the Commission submitted a substantive report to the General Assembly on confidence-building measures in the field of conventional arms. On another encouraging note, the Secretary-General's Advisory Board on Disarmament Matters concluded its two-year programme of work on the topic of global military spending, presenting a set of practical proposals aimed at curbing and reversing the upward trend of expenditure.

With respect to the First Committee of the General Assembly, the year saw record-high levels of participation, a growing number of votes on resolutions—148 in total—and a consistent trend of competing draft resolutions

Figure 7.1
From consensus to contention: tracking shifts in the General Assembly's disarmament decision-making over the years

Number of resolutions and decisions by type of adoption as a whole, 2010–2023

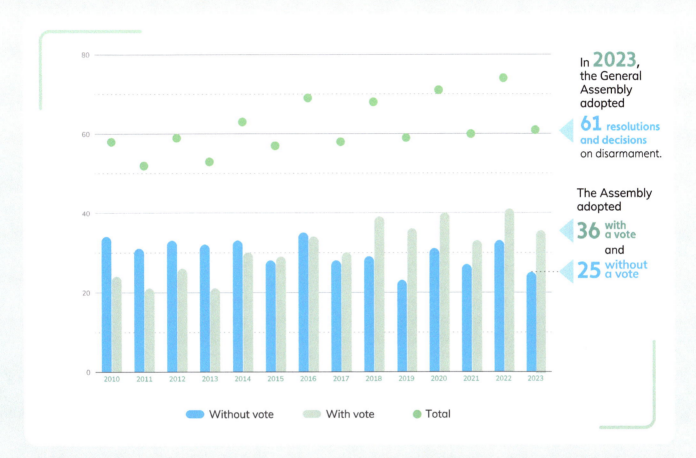

When the General Assembly cannot unanimously agree to adopt a proposed resolution or decision, Member States can instead do so by a vote. The graph shows that, since 2017, the General Assembly has voted on the majority of its disarmament-related resolutions and decisions each year, reversing a prior trend of collective agreement on most of its adopted texts. The graph also reveals that the General Assembly has adopted more disarmament texts in recent years, partly due to States tabling competing resolutions on the same issue.

being tabled under the same agenda item. Discussions in the Committee were tense, with heated exchanges on the wars in Ukraine and Gaza, as well as other hotspots, such as the Korean Peninsula and Nagorno-Karabakh. Many States lamented the deteriorating international security environment, which was partly reflected in heightened nuclear weapons-related rhetoric, security challenges emanating from new domains in cyber and outer space, and the negative consequences of the proliferation of illicit small arms and light weapons.

Overall, the First Committee considered a total of 60 draft resolutions and one decision, a decrease from the previous session. The First Committee also voted on two draft amendments, which the sponsors of the respective resolutions deemed "hostile". Three new resolutions were adopted by vote, namely those on the topics of radiological weapons, the legacy of nuclear weapons and related victims' assistance and remediation, and lethal autonomous weapons systems.

Meanwhile, States continued to express deep frustration over the ongoing stalemate in the Conference on Disarmament. That body once again remained unable to agree to a programme of work, despite efforts towards consensus undertaken by the first three presidencies of the 2023 session under Egypt, Ethiopia and Finland. In the absence of a programme of work, the presidencies convened formal and informal thematic plenaries under the agenda items of the Conference, enabling States members to discuss a variety of specific topics, including nuclear-weapon-free zones, disarmament and gender in the context of the women, peace and security agenda, the responsible use of AI in the military domain and the disarmament aspects of the vision presented in *A New Agenda for Peace*. Those States also considered "the improved and effective functioning of the Conference" after taking up the matter at an informal retreat organized by UNIDIR, held in June, with support from the presidencies of France and Germany. Later in the year, the Hungarian presidency secured consensus on a comprehensive final procedural report, as well as a return to consensus on the annual resolution adopted at the seventy-eighth session of the General Assembly, First Committee. However, in an unprecedented development, the Conference was not able to take any decision on the participation of non-States members, due to disagreements on the procedure for approving such requests.

A bright spot of 2023 was the Disarmament Commission's submission of a substantive report to the General Assembly at its seventy-eighth session (A/78/42). Based on discussions in its Working Group II, the Commission adopted, by consensus, recommendations to promote the practical implementation of transparency and confidence-building measures in outer space activities with the goal of preventing an arms race in outer space, in accordance with the recommendations set out in the report of the Group of Governmental Experts on Transparency and Confidence-Building Measures in Outer Space Activities. Unfortunately, for the nineteenth consecutive year, there were no consensus recommendations put forward for the agenda item "Recommendations for achieving the objective of nuclear disarmament and non-proliferation of nuclear weapons", allocated to Working Group I of the Commission.

In its final report (A/78/287), the Advisory Board on Disarmament Matters provided a set of practical and concrete proposals to curb and reverse the upward trend in military spending,[1] centred around the belief that a more holistic conception of security is needed. To achieve that vision, the Board sought to identify three complementary pathways with associated actions at a time when new insights and energy were sorely needed. Those three pathways were centred on (a) encouraging critical, innovative and transformative thinking about military spending; (b) lessening threat perceptions and risk escalation and reducing military spending; and (c) strengthening analysis, data collection and public awareness.

---

[1] Global military expenditure reached an all-time high of $2.4 trillion in 2023, according to an analysis by the Stockholm International Peace Research Institute.

OPPOSITE PAGE: Since its inception in 1978, the Advisory Board on Disarmament Matters (ABDM) has made steady progress towards gender parity. As of 2023, there are eight women and seven men on the Board. The Secretary-General chooses the members of the Board from all regions of the world for their knowledge and experience in the field of disarmament and international security. Members serve in their personal capacity and are active in various fields—diplomacy (whether active or retired), civil society and academia. Sustained efforts are ongoing to ensure broad and equitable geographical representation.

Figure 7.2
Advisory Board on Disarmament Matters: a diverse body of experts

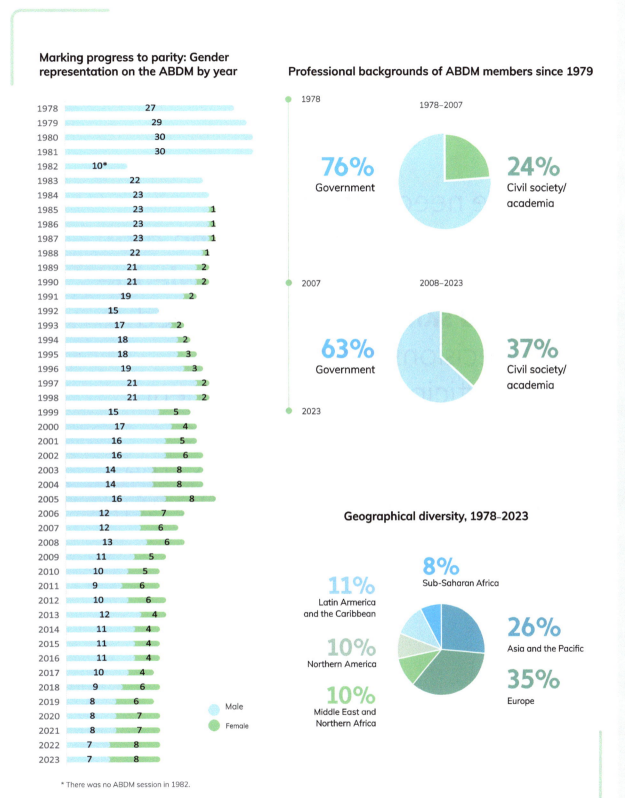

* There was no ABDM session in 1982.

We need **critical and empowered citizens** who are equipped **with the knowledge and skills** to make informed decisions, meaningfully participate in disarmament efforts and contribute to policymaking processes. The disarmament community of the future is being built today.

Izumi Nakamitsu
High Representative for Disarmament Affairs

8 Information and outreach

Leaders to the Future visit the Vienna International Centre to present youth insights for strengthening the nuclear non-proliferation and disarmament regime, during an event held on the margins of the Nuclear Non-Proliferation Treaty Preparatory Committee session from 31 July to 11 August.

INFORMATION
and outreach

In 2023, the General Assembly adopted its biennial resolution on youth, disarmament and non-proliferation (resolution 78/31), reaffirming the important and positive contribution that young people could make to the promotion and attainment of sustainable peace and security.

Meanwhile, the Office for Disarmament Affairs launched a new and innovative programme called the "Youth Leader Fund for a World Without Nuclear Weapons", offering 100 scholarships to young people from 63 countries. In December, those participants set out on a journey designed to hone their knowledge, skills and networks as nuclear disarmament advocates, through online courses on nuclear disarmament, non-proliferation and arms control, as well as practical skills training. The scholarship programme focused on lessons that the hibakusha—survivors of the atomic bombings of Hiroshima and Nagasaki—have long shared with the world about the unimaginable suffering that nuclear weapons caused.

For the forty-seventh consecutive year since 1976, the Office for Disarmament Affairs published the *United Nations Disarmament Yearbook*, a comprehensive source of information on global disarmament, non-proliferation and arms control efforts. A new, graphically enhanced preview edition was made available in July, while a comprehensive account of developments and issues in the field of disarmament was issued later in the year. For the first time, the *Yearbook* was made available in its entirety in *website* form. Moreover, the Office launched the revamped *Disarmament Resolutions and Decisions Database*, a user-friendly online tool with disarmament resolutions, decisions and voting patterns of the General Assembly. Likewise, the latest details on current disarmament treaties and agreements were made available in the redesigned *Disarmament Treaties Database*.

Seeking to strengthen the sustainability and impact of its disarmament education efforts, the Office held a global launch of its first formal Disarmament Education Strategy, in March. In line with the Strategy, the Office prioritized partnerships in its educational activities throughout the year, working with diverse United Nations entities, civil society partners and think tanks to conduct outreach and education activities. For example, the Office organized interactive exhibitions and movie screenings at various moments of the year to showcase disarmament and its linkages to human rights and development. Specifically, it held events marking the occasions of the thirtieth anniversary of the Vienna Declaration and Programme of Action (25 June), the Disarmament Week (24–30 October) and the International Human Rights Day (10 December). In addition, the Office's *Disarmament Education Dashboard*, featuring self-paced short courses on salient disarmament issues, achieved an all-time high of 25,774 registered users.

The Office also produced a new edition of its Civil Society and Disarmament collection, entitled *The Historical Impact of Parliamentary Diplomacy on Disarmament*. In the publication, the authors examined the key role of parliamentary diplomacy in foreign affairs, in particular its influence in the field of disarmament. They also outlined good practices and effective strategies with respect to parliamentary diplomacy, concluding with a set of specific policy recommendations.

In 2023, the Office redesigned the yearly publication *Programmes Financed from Voluntary Contributions*, with the 2022–2023 edition published in December as a web-only publication with an improved, easy-to-read format. The report showcased concrete results of its partnerships with donors and underscored the essential role of extrabudgetary support in attaining important disarmament goals.

Over the course of the year, the Office produced three titles under its Occasional Papers series. The first, *The Global Reported Arms Trade: Transparency in Armaments Through the United Nations Register of Conventional Arms – A Guide to Assist National Points of Contact in Submitting Their National Reports* (No. 39), was released in April on the occasion of the thirtieth anniversary of the United Nations Register of Conventional Arms. The next Occasional Paper, *The United Nations and Disarmament amid COVID-19: Adaptation and Continuity* (No. 40), explored how the COVID-19 outbreak posed an unprecedented challenge to intergovernmental disarmament institutions and processes. In December, the Office published Occasional Paper No. 41, *Celebrating 45 years of the Secretary-General's Advisory Board on Disarmament Matters: Creative, Inclusive, and Cooperative Diplomacy at Work*, highlighting the Board's contributions to advancing multilateral disarmament, its distinctive features and strengths, and its potential role in addressing the pressing challenges of today's world.

Figure 8.1
Empowering global youth: disarmament outreach by the United Nations in numbers

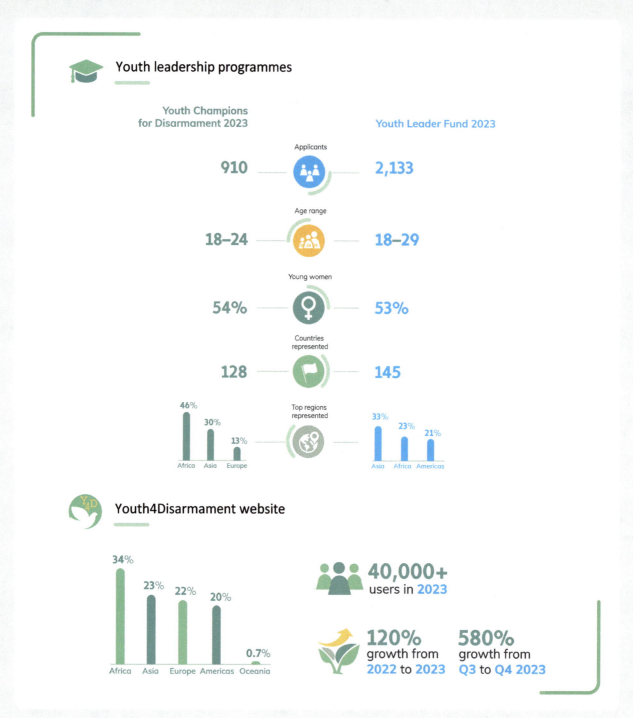

The key youth leadership programmes of the Office for Disarmament Affairs have successfully attracted and resonated with a diverse range of young individuals across regions. In line with the Office's commitment to demystifying disarmament, the programmes have also encouraged participation from youth with creative and non-traditional skillsets, thereby broadening access to the field.

The effectiveness of the Office's youth outreach efforts is evident through the diverse user base of the Youth4Disarmament website. For instance, in the last six months of 2023, the website reached individuals from over 192 countries, accessing content in more than 64 languages. The website has also been instrumental in garnering greater visibility and awareness regarding disarmament, non-proliferation and arms control among its audience.

NOTE: Locations sourced from the website have been matched to UN M49 Standard Country Codes for Statistical Use.

Figure 8.2
Charting progress: the global reach of online disarmament education

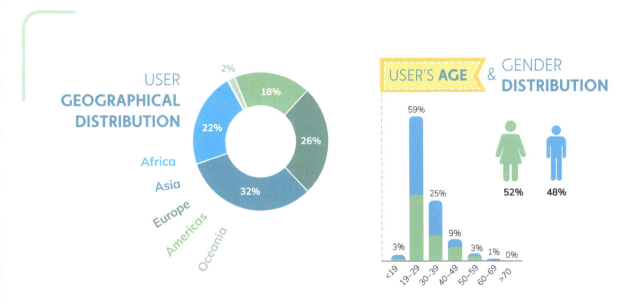

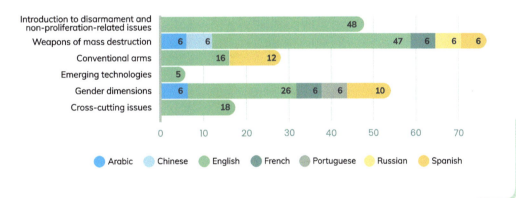

In 2023, the first year of the implementation of the Disarmament Education Strategy, the Vienna Office supported efforts to mainstream disarmament within broader educational initiatives and to connect with audiences where they are and on what matters most to them. For example, the Disarmament Education Dashboard, further reinvigorated by the Strategy, has registered almost twice as many users as in 2022, reaching all geographical regions of the United Nations.

The Disarmament Education Dashboard is an online learning platform providing free courses on disarmament to diverse audiences. It offers interactive, self-paced, instructor-led and blended courses, webinars and workshops, globally accessible from various devices.

The Disarmament Education Strategy

In December 2022, the Office for Disarmament Affairs launched its first Disarmament Education Strategy, which provides a common framework for the Office's disarmament education efforts, guided by an "inform, engage, educate and empower" approach. The objective of disarmament education is to impart knowledge and skills to individuals and to empower them to make their contributions, as informed national and world citizens, to the achievement of concrete disarmament and non-proliferation measures. Disarmament education prepares the next generation of leaders by enhancing knowledge and skills needed for young people to become agents of change.

A range of other practical disarmament publications were also launched, including the *Report of the Scientific Advisory Group on the Status and Developments Regarding Nuclear Weapons, Nuclear Weapon Risks, the Humanitarian Consequences of Nuclear Weapons, Nuclear Disarmament and Related Issues*, presented by the Advisory Group at the second Meeting of States Parties to the Treaty on the Prohibition of Nuclear Weapons.

The main website of the Office for Disarmament Affairs recorded over 634,000 unique visits in 2023. During the year, the Office upgraded the website to help improve its security, performance and reliability. Meanwhile, the Office launched its new Meetings Place portal, which provides a one-stop shop for documents and statements for multilateral disarmament meetings.

Regarding media outreach, the High Representative for Disarmament Affairs participated in press briefings and more than 30 interviews with international television, radio and print reporters. She also featured in a new Netflix documentary, *Unknown: Killer Robots*, on lethal autonomous weapons systems. The show explored the potential impacts of AI on the future of warfare and spotlights potential measures that could be taken to mitigate crucial risks to international peace and security.

The Office for Disarmament Affairs continued efforts to facilitate the diverse and inclusive engagement of young people in the disarmament and non-proliferation field through its #Youth4Disarmament outreach initiative. The Office launched the Leaders to the Future workshop series, empowering 55 young advocates to explore how disarmament, non-proliferation and arms control were linked with other topics related to the maintenance of international peace and security. Meanwhile, young people around the world participated in the annual #StepUp4Disarmament youth campaign by completing a distance of 8.29 km,

a symbolic number that corresponds with the date of the International Day against Nuclear Tests, on 29 August.

The United Nations Programme of Fellowships on Disarmament trained diplomats and other officials from 24 States.[1] Additionally, the United Nations–Singapore Cyber Fellowship was held again in 2023 to equip national authorities working on cyber strategy, policy, technology and operations, with practical knowledge and skills drawing upon the United Nations-developed normative framework.

UNIDIR, an autonomous research institute within the United Nations, undertook research activities under five multi-year programmes, on conventional arms and ammunition; weapons of mass destruction; gender and disarmament; security and technology; and space security. It produced a total of 96 publications. UNIDIR also deployed a redesigned website during the year, further boosting the reach and impact of its work, as well as expanding its offering of digital confidence-building tools through the launch of the Artificial Intelligence Policy Portal, the Space Security Portal, the Lexicon for Outer Space Security and the Biological Weapons Convention National Implementation Measures Database. Furthermore, UNIDIR pursued its bridge-building function by engaging in and facilitating dialogue between disarmament stakeholders through 148 conferences, workshops and events, which attracted over 11,000 participants.

---

[1] Armenia, Azerbaijan, Bahamas, Bahrain, Chile, China, Côte d'Ivoire, Czechia, Democratic Republic of the Congo, Germany, Japan, Lao People's Democratic Republic, Malawi, Maldives, Mexico, Morocco, Nepal, North Macedonia, Peru, Philippines, Romania, South Africa, the Sudan and Switzerland.

In January, the United Nations Regional Centre for Peace and Disarmament in Asia and the Pacific organized a workshop to strengthen disarmament education in Nepal, inviting educators in secondary and tertiary educational institutions across Nepal.

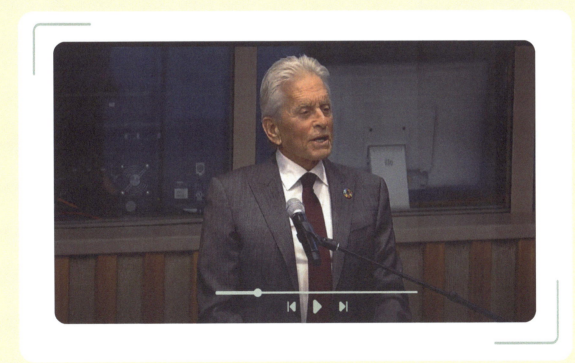

Michael Douglas delivers remarks at the International Day of Peace youth event

On 14 September, Michael Douglas, **United Nations Messenger of Peace**, delivered remarks at the youth event for the International Day of Peace. Celebrating his twenty-fifth anniversary as a United Nations Messenger of Peace, he shared his personal motivation for supporting the United Nations' work on nuclear disarmament.

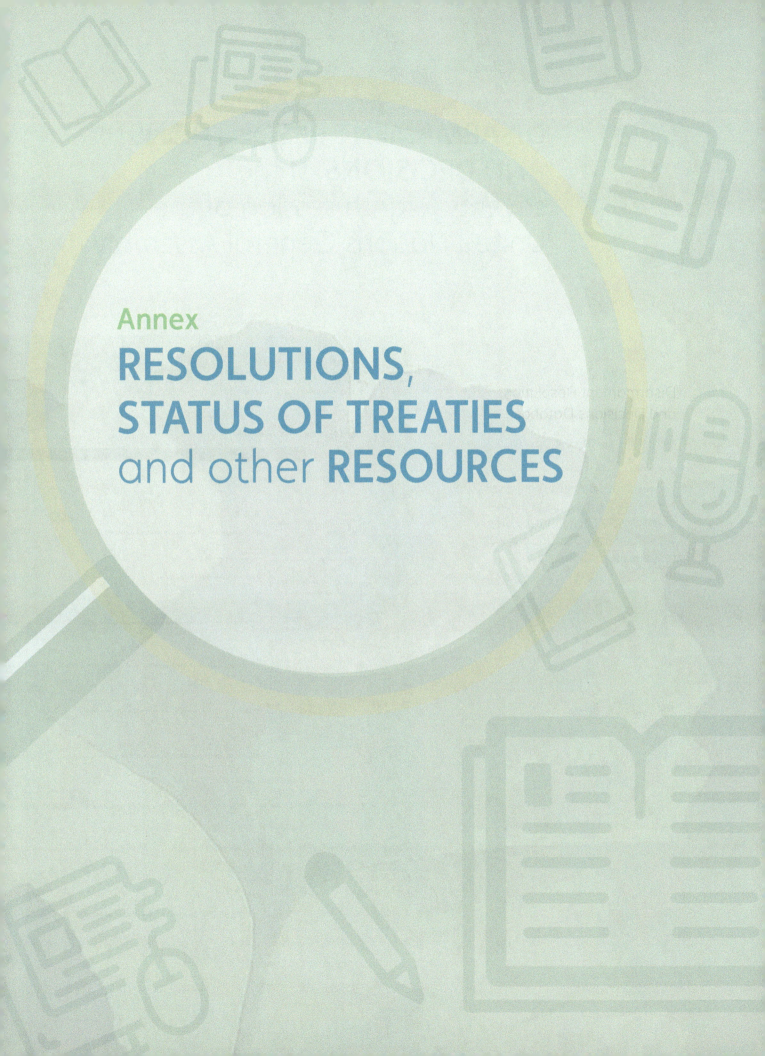

Annex
RESOLUTIONS, STATUS OF TREATIES and other RESOURCES

DISARMAMENT RESOLUTIONS AND DECISIONS of the seventy-eighth session of the United Nations General Assembly

Disarmament Resolutions and Decisions Database

https://resolutions.unoda.org

The revamped database's improved features make it simple to pinpoint specific votes and track State voting patterns. Data for previous sessions are forthcoming.

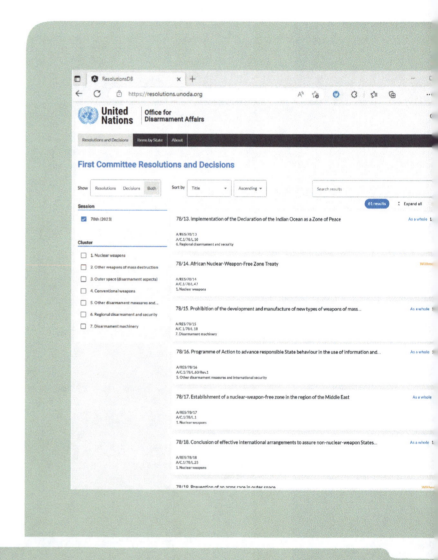

Status of multilateral arms regulation and DISARMAMENT AGREEMENTS

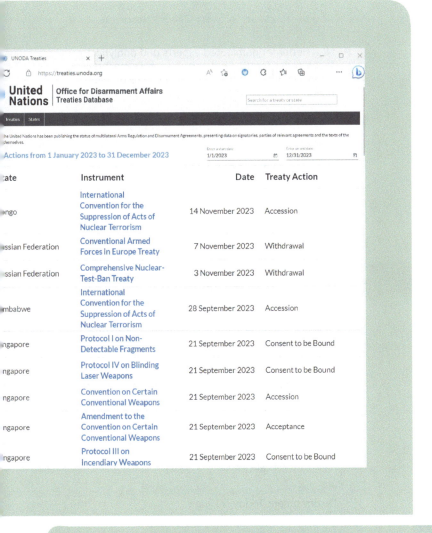

Disarmament Treaties Database

https://treaties.unoda.org

The redesigned database is easy to search with new filters and a user-friendly interface.

PUBLICATIONS and other INFORMATION MATERIALS in 2023

United Nations Office for Disarmament Affairs

Publications

- *United Nations Disarmament Yearbook 2022*, vol. 47 (condensed and full versions): (Sales No. E.23.IX.3)
- *The Global Reported Arms Trade: Transparency in Armaments Through the United Nations Register of Conventional Arms – A Guide to Assist National Points of Contact in Submitting Their National Reports*, Occasional Papers, No. 39 (Sales No. 23.IX.1)
- *The United Nations and Disarmament amid COVID-19: Adaptation and Continuity*, Occasional Papers, No. 40 (Sales No. E.23.IX.2)
- *Celebrating 45 Years of the Secretary-General's Advisory Board On Disarmament Matters: Creative, Inclusive, and Cooperative Diplomacy at Work*, Occasional Papers, No. 41 (Sales No. E.24.IX.1)
- *The Historical Impact of Parliamentary Diplomacy on Disarmament*, Civil Society and Disarmament 2023 (Sales No. E.24.IX.2)
- *Programmes Financed from Voluntary Contributions, 2022–2023*
- *Guide to Implementing the Biological Weapons Convention* (in Arabic, Chinese, English, French, Russian, Spanish and Portuguese)
- *Resolution 1540 and the African Continental Free Trade Area: Policy Options to Strengthen Non-proliferation Controls and Secure Trade*
- *Scientific and Technological Developments: Benefits and Risks for the Biological Weapons Convention* (conference report on supporting the full and effective implementation of Security Council resolution 1540 (2004) in Africa)
- *Report of the Scientific Advisory Group on the Status and Developments Regarding Nuclear Weapons, Nuclear Weapon Risks, the Humanitarian Consequences of Nuclear Weapons, Nuclear Disarmament and Related Issues* (TPNW/MSP/2023/8)
- *Supporting the Full and Effective Implementation of United Nations Security Council Resolution 1540 (2004) in Africa*
- Newsletter for nominated experts and analytical laboratories for the Secretary-General's mechanism for investigation of alleged use of chemical and biological weapons (*No. 5 (February 2023)* and *No. 6 (September 2023)*)
- *UNODA[1] Updates* (online news updates)

E-learning courses

- "*Treaty on the Non-Proliferation of Nuclear Weapons (NPT)*" (self-paced)
- "*Gender-mainstreaming Small Arms Control Training Course*" (self-paced, available in English, French, Spanish and Portuguese)
- "*Youth Leader Fund for a World Without Nuclear Weapons*" (instructor-led)
- "*Disarmament Toolkit*" (2023 edition)
- "Interdicting Small Arms, Ammunition, Parts and Components Course" (instructor-led; in English and Spanish)
- "Course on Combating Trafficking in Arms and Ammunition (CTAM)" (instructor-led; in Spanish)
- "Specialized Course on Firearms Investigations from a Gender Perspective" (instructor-led)

Podcasts

- "*Explosive Weapons In Populated Areas*", Disarmament Today, 21 June
- "*Bridging the divide: the role of networks in advancing inclusive disarmament processes*", Vienna Conversation Series, 6 September

---

[1] United Nations Office for Disarmament Affairs.

Publications and other information materials

- "Not so peaceful technology? What risks may civilian AI pose to peace and security?", Responsible AI for Peace Podcast (episode 1), 10 October
- "With Emily Bender, on risks of large language models and generative AI", Responsible AI for Peace Podcast (episode 2), 14 December

Videos

- Various video-recorded remarks of Izumi Nakamitsu, High Representative for Disarmament Affairs, available from the Office for Disarmament Affairs YouTube channel
- Highlights of the virtual launch event of International Day for Disarmament and Non-Proliferation Awareness, 4 March
- Video to mark International Women's Day 2023: "ODA celebrates the many women contributing to a more secure and peaceful cyberspace", 8 March
- Video to launch the online self-paced course on gender-mainstreaming small arms control, 8 March
- "International Day for Disarmament and Non-Proliferation Awareness | Launch", 9 March
- Opening remarks of United Nations Secretary-General António Guterres at the fifth Review Conference of the Chemical Weapons Convention, 15 May
- United Nations Messenger of Peace Michael Douglas calls on young people to become changemakers for a world free of nuclear weapons, 18 May
- Video on the adoption of the Global Framework on Through-Life Conventional Ammunition Management, 9 June
- "What is the United Nations Office for Disarmament Affairs?", 14 June
- Video featuring United Nations Messenger of Peace Michael Douglas on human rights and disarmament, 27 June
- Video to call for applications to the Youth Leader Fund training programme, 7 July
- Video on civilians as casualties of explosive weapons in populated areas, 18 July
- "What is the Disarmament Yearbook?", 24 July
- "What is the Treaty on the Non-Proliferation of Nuclear Weapons?", 25 July
- Video on chapter 1 (Nuclear disarmament and non-proliferation) of the 2022 Disarmament Yearbook, 26 July
- Video on chapter 2 (Biological and chemical weapons) of the 2022 Disarmament Yearbook, 27 July
- Video on chapter 3 (Conventional weapons) of the 2022 Disarmament Yearbook, 28 July
- "What happens at the Treaty on the Non-Proliferation of Nuclear Weapons First Preparatory Committee meeting?", 30 July
- Video on chapter 4 (Regional disarmament) of the 2022 Disarmament Yearbook, 30 July
- "Young people as contributors to a safer, more secure and equitable world through disarmament", 12 August
- "Side event on youth insights to first Preparatory Meeting for the 2026 NPT Review Conference", 24 August
- "Congratulatory message to participants of the #StepUp4Disarmament Youth Campaign 2023", 30 August
- "Leaders to the Future participate in #StepUp4Disarmament Youth Campaign 2023", 8 September
- "United Nations Messenger of Peace, Michael Douglas delivers remarks to International Day of Peace Youth Event", 15 September
- "Michael Douglas, Messenger of Peace, message on the International Day for the Total Elimination of Nuclear Weapons", 26 September
- "Michael Douglas, Messenger of Peace - Disarmament Week 2023", 25 October
- The 2023 Youth for Biosecurity Fellows share their experience of the Fellowship, 31 October
- Naomi Ekpoki, a United Nations Youth Champion for Disarmament 2020-2022, talks about her experience with the 1st edition of the training programme, 2 November
- "Michael Douglas reflects on the Political Declaration on Explosive Weapons in Populated Areas", 18 November
- Video to mark the first anniversary of the adoption of the Political Declaration on Strengthening the Protection of Civilians from the Humanitarian Consequences Arising from the Use of Explosive Weapons in Populated Areas, 18 November (created by the United Nations Office for the Coordination of Humanitarian Affairs and utilized by UNODA and other partner entities)

United Nations Institute for Disarmament Research

Conventional arms and ammunition

Publications

- *Weapons and Ammunition Management Country Insight: Central African Republic* (in English and French)
- *Strengthening Shared Understanding on the Impact of the ATT in Addressing Risks of Diversion in Arms Transfers: A Compendium of Key Resources and Tools* (in English, French and Spanish)
- *Weapons and Ammunition Management - Country Insight Series: Togolese Republic* (in English and French)
- *The Role of Industry in Responsible International Transfers of Conventional Arms*
- *Uncrewed Aerial, Ground, and Maritime Systems: A Compendium*
- *Peacekeeping in Hostile Environments: The Impact of Illicit Arms on MINUSMA*
- *The Role of Industry and Other Private Sector Actors in Efforts To Counter the Diversion of Conventional Arms*
- *Technologies to Counter the Diversion of Small Arms and Light Weapons, and Components of Conventional Weapons*
- *Towards a Comprehensive Security Approach to Military Spending*
- *Weapons and Ammunition Management in Africa Insight: 2023 Update*

Other publications

- "*Is it time to reassess national security spending?*", Stockholm International Peace Research Institute, April
- "*Can arms and ammunition flows data inform conflict early warning and early response?*", Medium, 5 May

Gender and disarmament

Publications

- *Enfoques de Género en la Ciberseguridad: Diseño, Defensa y Respuesta* (in Spanish)
- *Actualización del Sistema: Hacia una Agenda de Mujeres, Paz y Ciberseguridad* (in Spanish)
- *Best Practices for Promoting Gender Equality in Conventional Arms Control: Survey Results*
- *Addressing Weapons in Conflict-Related Sexual Violence: The Arms Control and Disarmament Toolbox* (in English and French)
- *Gender and Diversity in the Convention on Cluster Munitions (CCM)*
- *Gender and Diversity in the Anti-Personnel Mine Ban Convention (APMBC)*
- *Beyond Oslo: Taking Stock of Gender and Diversity Mainstreaming in the Anti-Personnel Mine Ban Convention*

Journal and working group papers

- "*Taking forward gender mainstreaming efforts in the Nuclear Non-Proliferation Treaty*", working paper submitted to the Nuclear Non-Proliferation Treaty Preparatory Committee (NPT/CONF.2026/PC.I/WP.25)

Other publications

- "*5 ways that arms control and disarmament can help to prevent sexual violence in conflict*", Medium, 5 March
- "*Sexual violence in conflict and weapons: unpacking the links for better prevention*", International Committee of the Red Cross (blog), 28 September

Security and technology

Publications

- *Towards Responsible AI in Defence: A Mapping and Comparative Analysis of AI Principles Adopted by States*
- *Wading Murky Waters: Subsea Communications Cables and Responsible State Behaviour* (in Arabic, Chinese, English, French, Russian and Spanish)
- *Uncrewed Aerial, Ground, and Maritime Systems: A Compendium*
- *Towards a More Stable and Secure ICT Environment: Unpacking Inter-State Cooperation*
- *The 2022 Innovations Dialogue: AI Disruption, Peace and Security (Conference Report)*
- *Proposals Related to Emerging Technologies in the Area of Lethal Autonomous Weapons Systems: A Resource Paper (Updated)*
- *Operationalizing a Directory of Points of Contact for Cyber Confidence-Building Measures*
- *Unpacking Cyber Capacity-Building Needs: Part I. Mapping the Foundational Cyber Capabilities* (in English, Spanish and Portuguese)

Publications and other information materials

- *Unpacking Cyber Capacity-Building Needs: Part II. Introducing a Threat-Based Approach* (in English, Spanish and Portuguese)
- *Use of ICTs by States: Rights and Responsibilities Under the UN Charter*
- *Drawing Parallels: A Multi-Stakeholder Perspective on the Cyber PoA Scope, Structure and Content*
- *Artificial Intelligence Beyond Weapons: Application and Impact of AI in the Military Domain*
- *AI and International Security: Understanding the Risks and Paving the Path for Confidence-Building Measures*
- *Exploring Synthetic Data for Artificial Intelligence and Autonomous Systems: A Primer*

Weapons of mass destruction

Publications

- *Preparing for Success at the Fifth Review Conference of the Chemical Weapons Convention: A Guide to the Issues* (in English, with executive summaries in Arabic, Chinese, French, Russian and Spanish available)
- *The Past and Future of Bilateral Nuclear Arms Control*
- *Menzingen Verification Experiment: Verifying the Absence of Nuclear Weapons in the Field*
- *Revitalizing the Conference on Disarmament: Workshop Report* (in English and French)
- *Verifying the BWC: A Primer*
- *Reflections on Review Conferences: the Non-Proliferation Treaty, the Biological Weapons Convention and the Chemical Weapons Convention*

Journal and working group papers

- "*What's next? The ninth biological weapons Review Conference and beyond*"
- "Consideration of Gender in the GGE on Nuclear Disarmament Verification" (GENDVF/2023/WP.10)
- "*What we learned from recent calls for a Russian nuclear attack*", Carnegie Endowment for International Peace, 20 July
- "*Verifying the absence of nuclear weapons – results of a field exercise*", Institute of Nuclear Materials Management
- "*Ядерная несдержанность. Что показал спор о превентивном ударе по Западу*", Carnegie Endowment for International Peace, 11 July (in Russian)

- "An illustrative compendium of proposals submitted to the Conference on Disarmament" (CD/2328, annex II) (in Arabic, Chinese, English, French, Russian, Spanish)
- *Strategic Stability in Outer Space After Russia's Invasion of Ukraine*, Center for Naval Analyses, October

Other publications

- "*Biological Weapons Convention negotiations*", Geneva Policy Outlook, 30 January
- "*Developing a plan B for the Chemical Weapons Convention 5th Review Conference*", European Leadership Network, 9 May
- "*Preparing for success at the fifth Chemical Weapons Convention Review Conference*", 28 April

Space security

Publications

- *2022 Outer Space Security Conference Report*
- *Commercial Actors and Civil Society Consultation Report: How Can Non-Governmental Entities Contribute to Reducing Threats to Outer Space Systems?*
- *African Perspectives for Advancing Space Security Through Norms, Rules and Principles of Responsible Behaviours: Workshop Summary Report*
- *Constant Vigilance? Verification and Monitoring for Space Security (Space Dossier 8)*
- *A Lexicon for Outer Space Security* (in Arabic, Chinese, English, French, Russian and Spanish)
- *To Space Security and Beyond: Exploring Space Security, Safety, and Sustainability Governance and Implementation Efforts, Space Dossier 9*
- *2023 Outer Space Security Conference Report*

Journal and working group papers

- "*The role of norms, rules and principles of responsible behaviour for space security*", working paper submitted by UNIDIR (A/AC.294/2023/WP.3)
- "*Commercial Space Operators on the Digital Battlefield*", Centre for International Governance Innovation
- "*The Cyber Phantom Menace to Space Security*", Centre for International Governance Innovation

- "Not a rose by any other name: Dual-use and dual-purpose space systems", Lawfare, 5 June
- "Current trends and developments in outer space", working paper for the Group of Governmental Experts on Further Practical Measures for the Prevention of an Arms Race in Outer Space
- "Security, including vectors of threats"
- "The open-ended working group on reducing space threats through norms, rules and principles of responsible behaviours: The Journey so far, and the road ahead", *Air and Space Law*, vol. 48, special issue

Middle East weapons of mass destruction-free zone

Publications

- *Examining Modalities for Nuclear Disarmament in the Middle East WMD-Free Zone Treaty*
- *The Consultations in Glion and Geneva: A View from the Negotiating Table* (editions by Jeremy Issacharoff, Wael Al Assad, Jaakko Laajava, Angela Kane, Mikhail Ulyanov and Thomas Countryman)
- *Development and Cooperation on Nuclear Research and Energy in the Middle East: Workshop Report*
- *Middle East WMD Free Zone Project: Final Report*
- *Addressing Chemical and Biological Weapons Challenges Through the Middle East Weapons of Mass Destruction-Free Zone: Workshop Report*
- *Narratives of the Middle East WMD-Free Zone: Drivers, Themes and Historical Accounts*

Managing exits from armed conflict

Publications

- *How Rank Affects the Transition to Civilian Life: Lessons from the Reintegration Process in Colombia,* Findings Report 27
- *Coming Home: The Return and Reintegration of Families with Perceived ISIL Affiliation in Iraq,* Findings Report 28
- *The Prospects for Remote Assessment: A Comparison of Phone vs In-Person Interviews in Nigeria,* Findings Report 29
- *Understanding Receptivity to Returning Former Boko Haram Associates Through a Gender Lens,* Findings Report 30
- *Child Exits from Armed Groups in the Lake Chad Basin,* Findings Report 31
- *Return and Reintegration Prospects for Iraqis Coming Back From Al Hol,* Findings Report 32
- *Partners in Research: Participatory Research Training Pilot with Young People in Mosul, Iraq*
- *An Unfiltered View of Struggling to Find Peace: Photography Programme Pilot with Young People in Mosul, Iraq*
- *Factors Influencing Community Receptivity of Former Fighters in Somalia*
- *MEAC Conflict Exits Assessment Framework*
- *Understanding Factors Driving Weapons Holding in the North East of Nigeria*

EVENTS HELD ON THE MARGINS of the 2023 session of the FIRST COMMITTEE

2 October
- Responsible artificial intelligence in the military domain (organized by the permanent missions of the Kingdom of the Netherlands and the Republic of Korea)

5 October
- Creating an environment for nuclear disarmament (organized by the Permanent Mission of the United States)

10 October
- A declaration to prevent harm: strengthening the protection of civilians from explosive weapons in populated areas (organized by the permanent missions of Ireland and Norway, with the United Nations Office for Disarmament Affairs)
- Mapping and addressing the security risks arising from military uses of artificial intelligence (organized by the Permanent Mission of Pakistan)
- IEDs - What lessons can be learnt from other mass explosive incidents and be applied to hotspots where IEDs are prevalent? (organized by the Permanent Mission of France)

11 October
- The International Partnership for Nuclear Disarmament Verification (organized by the Permanent Mission of the United States)
- Explosive weapons and the Arms Trade Treaty (organized by the United Nations Trust Facility Supporting Cooperation on Arms Regulation, the United Nations Office for Disarmament Affairs, and Action on Armed Violence)

13 October
- Preparing for the future of international peace and security (organized by the United Nations Institute for Disarmament Research)

16 October
- 10 years on from Syria's accession to the Chemical Weapons Convention (organized by the Permanent Mission of the United Kingdom)
- Publication launch: *The Application and Impact of Artificial Intelligence Beyond Weapons* (organized by the United Nations Institute for Disarmament Research)

17 October
- Addressing the threat posed by nuclear terrorism to international peace and security: EU support to the UN for the universalization and effective implementation of the International Convention for the Suppression of Acts of Nuclear Terrorism (organized by the United Nations Counter-Terrorism Centre)
- Autonomous weapons systems and human control – What are the challenges and how to overcome them? (organized by the Permanent Mission of Austria)
- Establishing an international agency for biological safety and security (organized by the Permanent Mission of Kazakhstan)
- Publication launch: *Risks of AI* (organized by the United Nations Institute for Disarmament Research)

18 October
- Autonomous weapons: state positions and trends in weapons systems (organized by the Permanent Mission of Belgium)
- Digital tools for disarmament: UNIDIR portals and databases (organized by the United Nations Institute for Disarmament Research)
- In the crosshairs? Addressing military drone use and proliferation (organized by the Permanent Mission of the Kingdom of the Netherlands, with PAX, the Stimson Center and the United Nations Institute for Disarmament Research)

Resources

	› Preventing the re-emergence of chemical weapons in the 21st century (concept note) (organized by the Organisation for the Prohibition of Chemical Weapons and the United Nations Office for Disarmament Affairs)
19 October	› Advocating for nuclear justice (organized by the permanent missions of Kazakhstan and Kiribati)
	› Working to strengthen the NPT review process (organized by the Non-Proliferation and Disarmament Initiative)
	› Regional consultations on the programme of action to advance responsible State behaviour in the use of information and communications technologies in the context of international security pursuant to General Assembly resolution 77/37 (organized by the permanent missions of Egypt and France, with the United Nations Office for Disarmament Affairs)
20 October	› Exploring the space-nuclear nexus (organized by the Stockholm International Peace Research Institute and the Permanent Mission of the Kingdom of the Netherlands)
	› Reducing space threats through norms, rules and principles of responsible behaviours: a new approach to preventing an arms race in outer space (organized by the Permanent Mission of the United Kingdom)
	› Military expenditures and arms transfers: from opacity to transparency (organized by the United Nations Institute for Disarmament Research, the United Nations Office for Disarmament Affairs and the Stimson Center)
	› Water and conflict: addressing water insecurity issues in fragile and conflict-affected countries (organized by the permanent missions of Slovenia, Spain and Switzerland, with PAX)
23 October	› The ATT Voluntary Trust Fund (VTF): How to apply for VTF funding (organized by the Permanent Mission of the United Kingdom and the Arms Trade Treaty Secretariat)
	› 10 years of EU Support for ATT implementation and universalization: taking stock and moving forward (organized by the European Union, in cooperation with the Federal Office for Economic Affairs and Export Control of Germany and Expertise France)
	› Generation Z(ero): role of youth in achieving a world without nuclear weapons (organized by the United Nations Office for Disarmament Affairs)
24 October	› Arms control and armed violence in island States: perspectives from the Caribbean (organized by the Permanent Mission of the United Kingdom)
	› Exploring the complementarity of existing approaches for the future of outer space security (organized by the United Nations Institute for Disarmament Research and the United Nations Office for Disarmament Affairs)
	› Achieving tangible cooperation and compliance to avert nuclear catastrophe (organized by the permanent missions of Austria and Kuwait)
	› The new Global Framework for Through-life Conventional Ammunition Management (organized by the Permanent Mission of Germany and the United Nations Office for Disarmament Affairs)
25 October	› Book launch: *It is Possible: A future Without Nuclear Weapons* (organized by the United Nations Office for Disarmament Affairs and the Permanent Mission of Austria)
	› SALIENT: the Saving Lives Entity trust facility (organized by the United Nations Development Programme and the United Nations Office for Disarmament Affairs)
26 October	› Remembering Mr. Jayantha Dhanapala, leader for disarmament (organized by the United Nations Institute for Disarmament Research)
1 November	› Between tradition and the law: artisanal firearm production in West Africa (organized by Small Arms Survey and the Permanent Mission of France)